The Serious Sides of Sex

Sex Medicine   Sex Law
Sex Ethics   Sex Psychology

RELATED TO
Sexual Behavior

Neville Blakemore & Neville Blakemore, Jr.
Series Editors
✠✠✠✠✠✠✠✠✠✠✠✠✠✠✠✠✠

The Nevbet Company, Louisville, Kentucky
✠✠✠✠✠✠✠✠✠✠✠✠✠✠✠✠✠

Grateful acknowledgement is made to the following for permission to use:

Excerpts from *The Columbia University College of Physicians and Surgeons Complete Home Medical Guide*, © 1985 G. S. Sharpe Communications and The Trustees of Columbia University in the City of New York, permission of Crown Publishers, Inc., New York.

Excerpts from *The 1988 Encyclopaedia Britannica Book of the Year*, © 1988 by Encyclopaedia Britannica, Inc., Chicago.

Excerpts from *Sexually Transmitted Diseases*, Second Edition, King K. Holmes et al., © 1990 by McGraw-Hill, New York.

Excerpts from *The Random House College Dictionary*, Revised Edition, © 1988 by Random House, New York.

Excerpts from *Webster's New World Dictionary*, Third College Edition, © 1988 by New World Dictionaries, a division of Simon & Schuster, New York.

Cover design by Mary Jean Kirtley.
Printed in the United States.

To order, write, FAX, or call:
The Nevbet Company
2843 Brownsboro Road
Louisville, Kentucky 40206
(502) 897-1664 Voice/FAX
(800) 332-5806

Library of Congress Catalog Card Number: 91-72213

ISBN 0-9627611-1-7

CONTENTS

THE SPECIALTY EDITORS

Medical   Stanley A. Gall, MD
                   Donald E. Baxter Professor and Chairman
                   Department of Obstetrics and Gynecology
                   The School of Medicine, University of Louisville
                   Louisville, Kentucky

                   Arthur H. Keeney, MD, DSc
                   Dean Emeritus
                   The School of Medicine, University of Louisville
                   Louisville, Kentucky

Legal   Robert L. Stenger, TheoD, JD
                   Professor
                   The School of Law, University of Louisville
                   Louisville, Kentucky

                   Michele H. Ubelaker, PhD, JD
                   Assistant Professor
                   The School of Law, University of Louisville
                   Louisville, Kentucky

Ethical   Wayne E. Oates, PhD
                   Professor of Psychiatry and Behavioral Science
                   Program of Ethical and Pastoral Counseling
                   The School of Medicine, University of Louisville
                   Louisville, Kentucky

Psychological Virginia T. Keeney, MD
                   Director, Program in Humanities and Medicine
                   Associate Director, Child Psychiatric Services
                   Department of Psychiatry and Behavioral Science
                   The School of Medicine, University of Louisville
                   Louisville, Kentucky

Each of the above Specialty Editors disclaims any responsibility for the accuracy of any material in this publication, other than the material prepared by him or her.

5

WHAT THIS BOOK IS ABOUT

Purpose

THE SERIOUS SIDES OF SEX presents facts for consideration—medical, legal, ethical, and psychological—relative to sexual behavior.

The book's purpose is to help the reader—male or female, young or old—to decide upon that personal sexual life-style most likely to achieve sexual satisfaction free from medical and legal worry, free from ethical regrets, and free from psychological hang-ups.

The book is not concerned with *how* to engage in sex; there are many excellent how-to books already available.

Writers

The text was composed by the Series Editors from information from recognized sources. It was edited in turn by each of the Specialty Editors—medical, legal, ethical, and psychological.

The Specialty Editors wrote their own notes to supplement the text.

Authority

THE SERIOUS SIDES OF SEX is authoritative.

All of its Specialty Editors have advanced degrees; they are university instructors; and in addition to teaching, four maintain independent practices in their fields. Most have published in professional journals; one has authored many books. All are active in their professional associations.

They have diverse religious affiliations and convictions.

Four are men; two are women. All are parents.

Language

To be informative, precise terms are necessary. Thus, the language in this book is explicit. Euphemisms are avoided.

Neutrality

The Editors try to be neutral on controversial matters; for example, regarding abortion, they present facts but express neither approval nor disapproval for abortion on demand.

Having presented the facts and few opinions, the Editors trust the reader to make sexual decisions according to his or her personal interests.

Text

The text contains basic information about sexual behavior and its important consequences, especially with respect to social diseases and pregnancy.

Disease-related information includes, but is not limited to: avoidance, symptoms, treatment, partner, and follow-up.

Pregnancy-related information includes, but is not limited to: incest, rape, full-term, contraception, and abortion.

Notes

The Specialty Editors' notes contain supplementary sex-related medical, legal, ethical, and psychological information. By design, the notes are often longer than the text itself.

Format

The text refers the reader to the notes. For example, at the appropriate place, the text cites the note entitled

MASTURBATION; and the note deals quite thoroughly with the medical, legal, ethical, and psychological considerations of the practice of masturbation. (There *is* a legal consideration: it cannot be legally performed in public!)

THE SERIOUS SIDES OF SEX's format of concise text, extensively noted, makes possible the conveyance of much information with great reader convenience. In the above example, if readers are not interested in masturbation, they read on in the text; if they are interested, they can learn, in the note, what physicians, lawyers, ethicists, and psychologists think about the subject.

Altogether there are 65 notes supplementing information in the text.

Such an assemblage of text and notes is believed to be unique.

Reference

An understanding of what the Editors are talking about is essential. To facilitate such understanding, a Glossary explaining their technical terms is supplied.

For the many readers who will refer to *THE SERIOUS SIDES OF SEX* for specific information from time to time, two indexes are included: the Index relating to text material, and a Note Index listing note subjects.

ASPECTS OF SEXUAL BEHAVIOR

Legal Aspects

There are hardly any aspects of sexual activity that do not implicate some legal rule.

Generally, the law protects the right of married persons to engage in heterosexual activity. The law protects as well the right of an adult to obtain and use contraceptive drugs and devices, to obtain a sexual sterilization operation, and to obtain an abortion of a non-viable fetus. Rights of minors (persons not yet 18) are more complex.

In other areas, a person may incur civil and criminal liabilities incident to engaging in sex. Certain types of sexual activity—rape (sexual intercourse with a non-consenting partner), sexual intercourse with a minor, incest (sexual intercourse with a relative), and prostitution—are crimes in all states. Other types of sexual activity—homosexual relations, oral sex, anal sex, adultery, and fornication (sexual intercourse by an unmarried person)—may be illegal in some states. Additionally, it is a crime in some states to have sexual intercourse when one is infected with a venereal disease and is aware of it.

The potential for civil liability arising from sexual behavior is considerable. If a child is conceived of a union, both the father and mother will have the legal obligation to support that child to its majority. The availability of accurate biological tests to determine paternity makes it difficult for biological fathers to deny their parental responsibilities to children born out of wedlock. Couples who cohabit may find that they have entered into a valid marriage with all the rights and responsibilities of that re-

11

lationship, or they may find that they have few of the rights and protections of spouses. A person may incur considerable financial liability for transmitting a venereal disease to his or her unsuspecting partner.

Laws relating to sexual activities and the family vary considerably from state to state. It is often surprising to people that activities as intimate as sexual relations can be the subject of so much legal interest and scrutiny. A person who desires to be fully informed of the consequences of his or her actions should therefore be acquainted with local laws before making a decision regarding a sexual activity with another.

Robert L. Stenger, TheoD, JD
Michele H. Ubelaker, PhD, JD

Ethical Aspects

A few generalities concerning the religious ethics of sexual behavior need to be kept in mind when considering a specific behavior.

First, the degree of religious devoutness influences dramatically what a person does sexually.

Devoutness can be measured by the following criteria:

1) How active is one in attending the activities of one's religious group?

2) How often does one read the sacred Scriptures of one's faith?

3) How regularly does one pray?

4) How often does one seek God's will when making a major decision in life?

Second, religions around the world have fundamentalist, moderate or conservative, and liberal groupings of followers. For example, individual Protestant groups tend to have fundamentalist, moderate-conservative, and liberal divisions. While there is often press coverage of the official Roman Catholic teaching on sexual matters, available evidence about practice by those who claim to be Roman Catholics is that there are also fundamentalist, moderate or conservative, and liberal groupings. Islam has the Shi'ites (fundamentalist), Sunnis (moderate), and the Sufis (mystic). Judaism has Orthodox, Conservative, and Reformed branches. Each of such groups interprets the original Scriptures with differing degrees of literalness.

Third, the generation of one's participation in a particular faith group often affects how seriously one takes the sexual teaching of the group. For example, the first person in a family to be a Bahai, a Catholic, or a Methodist, is likely to be zealous and scrupulous about the teaching of the group. On the other hand, a fourth or fifth generation member of a faith sometimes is a less zealous adherent to the rules and regulations of the faith group. Individual cases vary; one example to the contrary is that of some Orthodox Jews, who take their faith very seriously and who have practiced it for many generations.

Fourth, in the United States today the punishment or penalty that religionists exact from sexually delinquent followers is mainly the sense of personal guilt and social alienation. However, excommunication from the sacraments is not unusual; and ecclesiastical courts or ad hoc disciplinary panels are the polity of some religious groups. For example, a Methodist church conference may adjudicate whether or not ministers should be dismissed for sexual misconduct. However, personal guilt and social "shunning" are generally the extent of religious penalties for such delinquents.

Finally, in the United States with its constitutional separation of church and state, old religious sins which historically were punished by both church and state, are now punished primarily by the state. Secular courts and not the churches now mete out the main punishment for incest, prostitution, rape, and other transgressions.

Readers interested in extensive background material on religious ethics of sexual behavior are referred to E. Geoffrey Parrinder's *Sex in the World's Religions* (London: Sheldon, 1980). Readers seeking general information about the world's religions may find Houston Smith's *The Reli-*

gions of Man (New York: Harper & Row, 1986) useful. Finally, perhaps the best single volume for comprehensive coverage of world religions is *Abingdon Dictionary of Living Religions* (Nashville: Abingdon Press, 1981), Keith Crim, Editor.

Wayne E. Oates, PhD

Estimated Religious Population of the World

	North America		World	
Christians				
Roman Catholics	91,209,800	34.0	926,194,600	18.5
Protestants	94,965,500	35.4	332,016,400	6.6
Others	45,873,100	17.1	386,185,500	7.7
Total Christians	232,048,400	86.5	1,644,396,500	32.8
Muslims	2,682,600	1.0	860,388,300	17.2
Buddhists	190,000	0.1	309,626,100	6.2
Jews	8,084,000	3.0	18,075,400	0.4
Others	25,259,000	9.4	2,165,122,700	43.4
Total	268,264,000	100.0%	4,997,609,000	100.0%

Adapted with permission from *The 1988 Encyclopedia Britannia Book of the Year*, © 1988 by Encyclopedia Britannia, Inc.

Psychological Aspects

Some generalizations regarding psychology should be remembered, when considering the psychological notes in this book.

Psychological consequences depend on many factors and are extremely individualized. For example, people with over-developed consciences suffer more discomfort (anxiety, guilt, shame) over minor or even imagined infractions than do average people. But conversely, people with under-developed consciences, or with sociopathic traits, fully or partially developed, may feel little or no discomfort by performing generally disapproved or even illegal acts.

Parental training (which may take many forms, some expressed, some implied, with respect to adolescent expressions of sexuality) has a great impact on the developing person; the nature and content of such training has a large influence on individual differences. Also, since children observe and learn from parent-parent interactions—to love, to hate, to be indifferent, or whatever—these parental interactions become a part of the adult person.

Family moral attitudes, personality, conscience development, education, and experience all contribute to individual psychological variations. Societal norms and expectations contribute as well. Important psychological differences between males and females are considerations, as are the different expectations of sex that partners may or may not share.

There is constant professional debate about the relative importance of these many factors in forming the adult-to-be.

Readers seeking more information are referred to *The Family Book About Sexuality*, Revised Edition, by Mary S. Calderone and Eric W. Johnson (New York: Harper & Row, 1989), and to *Human Sexuality and Its Problems*, Second Edition, by John Bancroft (New York: Churchill Livingstone, 1989).

Virginia T. Keeney, MD

SEXUAL OPTIONS

There is no device or substance which will prevent the transmission of venereal diseases or sperm between sexually active males and females with absolute certainty.

For those who wish to avoid all worry and the inadvertent transmission of diseases and sperm, there are limited options in responding to the sexual drive. One is complete abstinence from sexual acts; such abstinence is called chastity, and sometimes celibacy, when referring to abstinence from sexual intercourse. See 1 ABSTINENCE. Abstaining males find relief naturally from nature's nocturnal emissions or wet dreams; abstaining females find such relief naturally from nocturnal orgasms. See 2 WET DREAMS & NOCTURNAL ORGASMS. Another response is masturbation which can be practiced by both males and females, alone or in couples, and which for many is a sufficient sexual expression. See 3 MASTURBATION.

However, most persons prefer to achieve sexual gratification by sexual intercourse; and many believe that the sexual relationship that is at once the most gratifying, and the most likely to be free from medical and legal worry, from ethical regrets, and from psychological hang-ups, is a relationship with but a single partner who is disease free; who can be trusted to remain so; and who shares similar views on sexual behavior and responsibilities.

Risks

A sexual relationship almost always involves risks of some kind—medical, legal, ethical, and/or psychological.

Married persons are perhaps subject to the fewest of such risks, if they share similar views about sexual behavior,

17

responsibilities, and having children. Even if they share such views, factors beyond their control may introduce some form of sexual dysfunction, for example, impotence. See 4 IMPOTENCE.

If sexual partners are cohabiting and unmarried, then legally there is a risk, namely, that one of the partners might claim palimony. See 5 PALIMONY. In some jurisdictions, cohabitation might become a common law marriage. See 6 COMMON LAW MARRIAGE.

Married or single, the chance of contracting or transmitting a venereal disease is greatly increased by promiscuous sexual activities; and the chance of an unwanted pregnancy is increased by having sexual intercourse with more than one partner. See 7 PROMISCUITY.

If the relationship is homosexual, homosexuals still run some risk of social opprobrium, although in many social circles there is increased acceptance of homosexuality. See 8 HOMOSEXUALITY. There are still legal and regulatory prohibitions against homosexual behavior. For example, homosexuals may encounter legal restrictions, such as denial of security clearances or enlistment or promotion in the military, denial of housing or employment, or even criminal prosecution. See 9 SECURITY.

There are other forms of sexual engagement in addition to intercourse. Regarding fellatio and cunnilingus, see 10 ORAL SEX; regarding sodomy or buggery, see 11 ANAL SEX; and regarding bestiality, see 12 BESTIALITY. While some of these forms are practiced with satisfaction by agreeing couples, nevertheless all involve risk of some kind.

---

1 ABSTINENCE

Medical

There are no proven negative medical consequences from the practice of sexual abstinence, for either the male or the female. It has been said that the continuing practice of sexual abstinence, or repressing desire, by females may lead to pelvic congestion syndrome, that is, an abnormal dilation of pelvic veins leading to an abnormal accumulation of fluid in the pelvic region. However, this has not been established medically.

Legal

In states in which divorce is granted on the basis of marital fault, courts have held that unjustified refusal of sexual intercourse would constitute cruelty and be a grounds for divorce. What constitutes justified refusal (e.g. spouse is intoxicated, prior physical or emotional abuse, unreasonably frequent requests for intercourse, request for unusual methods of intercourse) is decided by the court.

Divorce laws typically require that before a final decree can be entered the parties "must live separate and apart" for a period of time (sixty days to six months); parties may live "separate and apart" under this statute if they cohabit in the same residence without engaging in sexual intercourse (so as not to penalize those who could not afford to set up separate residences).

The law obliges those who know they have a sexually transmitted disease to abstain from sexual intercourse. They may be liable for criminal prosecution and for damages to one to whom they have transmitted the disease. See 19 DAMAGES.

Ethical

In Judaism, sexual abstinence outside of marriage is required. The reasons for this are: (1) that the virginity of women be protected (Exodus 22:17); and (2) that the Jewish people might be kept free of participating in the cultic sexual practices of alien peoples around them.

In Islam, sexual activity outside of marriage is to "commit indecency." (Koran 4, 20) Sexual activity outside of marriage is considered whoredom in the Sales translation of the Koran. Liberal provisions for the sexual needs of men and women are made in the marriage institutions of Islam.

In Buddhism, pre-marital or extramarital sex would be considered as a breach of the third of the Five Precepts of ethical behavior:

> To abstain from taking life.
> To abstain from taking what is not given.
> *To abstain from sexual immorality.*
> To abstain from false speech.
> To abstain from intoxicating liquors.

Celibacy is required of Buddhist priests.

In Christianity, failure to abstain from sex outside the bonds of marriage is considered to be fornication, promiscuity, or adultery. Abstinence within marriage is advised on a very limited and brief basis "in order to devote yourselves to prayer." (I Corinthians 7:5) Marital partners are admonished not to deny one another sexual access. Such denial is deemed a kind of spiritual fraud. In Catholicism, abstinence during the wife's time of fertility is taught as the only natural means of birth control and is the only one approved by the Church.

Celibacy is required of Catholic priests. In some instances, Anglican-Episcopal priests are celibate, but this seems to be voluntary and not required.

Psychological

Abstinence is an acceptable alternative, psychologically, to sexual intercourse, even for persons with strong sexual drives, if it is the considered choice of the individual, or of both members of a couple.

For those who want more of a sexual release than is provided naturally by wet dreams or nocturnal orgasms, means other than coitus may be substituted without negative psychological consequences.

2   WET DREAMS & NOCTURNAL ORGASMS

Medical

Males can rely on wet dreams as the only sexual release necessary for a natural, medically healthy sex life.

Females can rely on nocturnal orgasms (similar to the male's wet dreams) as the only sexual release necessary for a natural, medically healthy sex life.

Psychological

Wet dreams (nocturnal emissions) are natural in all males, especially pubescent and adolescent ones; such dreams are nature's way of relieving fluid in the seminal vesicles. When parents and child understand this, there is no reason for psychological reactions such as anxiety, shame, or guilt, which may ensue if the child's caretakers are punitive and harsh. The child's anxiety which could occur is based on guilt for having dreams that may involve, for example, forbidden sexual actions; or concern about loss of control; or fear of discovery and ensuing disapproval maybe accompanied by punishment; but such dreams accompanying the emissions are natural.

3   MASTURBATION

Medical

Masturbation does not create a medical problem for either males or females. The only potential problem is a state of mind that masturbation is harmful or immoral; there is no medical basis to justify such a state of mind.

Frequency of masturbation among those who so engage tends to decrease with age and among married persons.

"This normal, natural, and healthy activity begins in childhood continuing throughout life. The vast majority of Americans of both sexes and all ages masturbate, giving themselves pleasure and releasing sexual tensions. Many adolescents, however, feel guilty about the practice, especially since warnings and myths about masturbation seem to persist. Despite age-old myths, there is no evidence that masturbation is associated with hair falling out, pimples erupting, the onset of madness, or any other ill effect." (The Columbia University College of Physicians and Surgeons, *Complete Home Medical Guide*, [New York: Crown, 1985], 243)

Legal

Masturbation is not a crime if performed alone and in private. If it is in public, that is, in a place where the public might view it, it could be punished under a statute forbidding public indecency or indecent exposure. Homosexuals are arrested when police stake out areas where they gather and police find them exposing themselves or masturbating. If there is mutual masturbation, it may be a crime under a sexual contact statute which forbids touching the sexual organs of another for purposes of sexual gratification.

Ethical

In Judaism, the ethical literature heavily prohibits masturbation. The reason is that it is a waste of semen without intercourse with a woman. One rabbi equated it with adultery and lewdness, by means of the hand. The literature points to its supposed danger to health and warns of dire punishment in the day of reckoning. More liberal forms of Judaism today would not consider masturbation as a sin but as a form of sexuality that is a substitute for heterosexual intercourse, as a habit to be outgrown.

Islamic teaching prohibits masturbation because of the lewd fantasies that accompany it. It indicates a lack of mental discipline and inner wisdom.

Buddhism would focus on the way in which masturbation goes against the brief summation of Buddha's ethical teaching: "Avoid evil, do good, and purify the mind." The Noble Eightfold Path of ethical and spiritual discipline consists of right view, right aim, right speech, right action, right living, right effort, right mindfulness, and right concentration. Of these, right mindfulness calls for alert observation of the body aimed at the end of the craving and despair common in the world. Also, the right concentration that leads into Nirvana would be impossible with the attachments to the fantasies of masturbation.

In Christianity, the Catholic Church condemns masturbation because it avoids the responsibilities of sexual intercourse and the attendant possibility of procreation. Masturbation is considered unnatural. Strict, fundamentalist Protestant churches condemn the behavior as well.

However, moderate and liberal Catholics and Protestants would not consider masturbation a sin, but rather, much as in liberal Judaism, an unsatisfactory substitute for heterosexual intercourse to be outgrown as soon as heterosexual maturity is achieved. Pastoral counseling would be aimed at reducing the isolation and loneliness, the guilt, and shame a masturbator might feel.

None of the literature of religion makes reference to female masturbation insofar as the Ethical Editor has been able to determine.

Psychological

Sexual arousal of oneself, with or without the participation of another person, need not involve negative psychological sequelae. Despite the increasing societal acceptance of masturbation as normal rather than pathological, feelings of guilt from its practice are reported by many, and especially by females. On the other hand, some females report more satisfying orgasms from self-stimulation than with a partner, and for some females, masturbation may provide a satisfactory sexual outlet in the absence of a partner.

Condemnation of masturbation by upbringing or by religious belief which considers the practice sinful may induce psychological guilt.

Religious beliefs that semen is a source of strength which should not be wasted may make the practice especially guilt-producing.

Masturbation should be treated as a psychological emotional disorder when it is a form of exhibitionism, that is when done in public; or when preoccupation with masturbation interferes with the activities of normal life. Exhibitionism is believed to occur only with males; females, young or old, are almost always the victims.

Folklore about masturbation causing dire consequences, such as sterility or insanity, is unfounded.

Mutual masturbation is often the preferred sexual practice with homosexuals, either male or female.

4   IMPOTENCE
Medical

Impotence is the inability to perform sexual intercourse; it affects both sexes, but more often males.

Impotence may originate from mental or physical causes. Mental causes include stress, fatigue, or depression, or even anxiety and guilt originating in childhood. Physical causes include medications; hormonal imbalances; and some diseases, such as diabetes mellitus; or nerve damage from an accident; or drug or alcohol abuse.

Impotence tends to increase with advancing age, probably from lower levels of the male sex hormone, testosterone, or from a decreased blood supply to the pelvis.

Impotence is often curable. Comprehensive diagnosis, which ideally should include both partners, can first determine whether the cause is mental or physical. Thereafter, effective therapy may be undertaken by a physician or psychological counselor.

Penile implants, which artificially create an erection and thus facilitate intercourse, are sometimes prescribed for males made permanently impotent by disease or nerve damage. Such implants must be surgically installed.

Legal

Impotence is legally defined as the inability to consummate a marriage by sexual intercourse. Although impotence refers to physical inability to consummate, such inability may arise from psychic causes. Impotence may be absolute (with respect to all partners) or relative (with respect only to a particular partner).

If a party to marriage is impotent, the couple may seek a declaration that the marriage is invalid if they do so within the requisite time period, usually one year. Impotence is a ground for invalidity only if the other party does not know of its existence; where impotence is known before the marriage, the parties waive their ability to seek a declaration of invalidity on that ground.

Impotence is to be carefully distinguished from sterility, which refers to the inability to become a parent. Persons who are not impotent may be sterile. Sterility is not a ground for declaring a marriage invalid; however, concealment of the fact of sterility prior to the marriage may be such a ground.

Ethical

No religious ethical teachings explicitly refer to impotence; it is a "non-issue." However, in marital therapy, the Ethical Editor has found some instances of hostility producing premature ejaculation, and in some cases total impotence.

Psychological

Psychic factors are the most common causes of impotence (erectile dysfunction). These include fear of failure or of rejection, boredom or anger toward the partner, stress, fatigue, worry that his performance will not satisfy his partner's demands (which he may well have exaggerated in his imagination). Other factors are fear of contracting a disease or concern about a past illness, such as a heart attack. Anxiety is the most common cause of all, resulting in feelings of worry or apprehension instead of the pleasure of sexual arousal.

Many men experience transient episodes of impotence which do not become recurrent and are not considered a problem. When frequent failures occur, however, help should be sought from a physician or urologist as soon as possible. The longer impotence persists, the harder it is to cure.

Impotence is frustrating and humiliating for males, a blow to their self-esteems. As a result, depression may occur, complicating the existing anxieties, worries, and fears; and indeed, depression itself can be a cause of impotence.

Treatment for psychogenic impotence includes forms of psychotherapy, training, and techniques which are designed to enable the patient to enjoy his sexual activities free of the unpleasant emotions which inhibit erection. Books and video tapes may aid in the therapy.

Females are generally more sensitive to pain during intercourse than males, and such pain may result in an unsatisfactory sexual experience and initiate inhibition.

Inhibition may evidence itself as vaginismus, or spasm of the vaginal muscles, and vaginismus may be so severe as to prevent penile penetration. Vaginismus may be present from the first coital experience, or sometimes may be traced back to a single painful episode. In mild cases, treatment may be effective with simple psychotherapeutic techniques. More severe cases, or cases stemming from a more generalized cause, may make therapy more difficult. Females in general are more apt to complain of lack of interest or enjoyment of sex than of inability to perform.

5 PALIMONY

Legal

The term "palimony" entered the American vocabulary in 1976 after the Supreme Court of California determined that Michelle Marvin could sue Lee Marvin for a share of property after their six years of unmarried cohabitation. Since the cohabitants had never married, their property could not be divided under laws for community property or equitable division of property acquired during marriage. Rather, a cohabitant must base a claim upon contract, trust, joint venture, partnership, or some other recognized legal or equitable basis.

A cohabitant could recover only if all of the requisite proof was produced. In the Marvin case, Michelle got nothing for she could not prove contract, trust, or any other legal or equitable basis for recovery.

Courts have been slow to recognize property claims by cohabitants, often because their words to each other, e.g. "I'll always take care of you," were not intended by the speaker to create a legal liability or because what was furnished to the other in goods or services is presumed in law to be a gift (as transfers between family members are often deemed gifts without requirement for payment).

Cohabitants have been successful in obtaining palimony, either in the form of a division of property or in the form of support for a period of time, where the court has found that refusing support would provide one party with an unjust enrichment or windfall at the expense of the other and it would be inequitable to allow the unjustly enriched party to so profit.

Palimony claims against the estate of a deceased cohabitant have been even less successful either on the grounds that the will is the only recognized way to pass property at death to people other than one's statutory heirs (and nowhere is a cohabitant who is not married to the decedent an heir) or that courts will not enforce contracts against makers whose mouths are closed by death and who cannot defend themselves against the survivor's claims and allegations.

6   COMMON LAW MARRIAGE
Medical
There are no medical risks involved in a common law marriage relationship, for the male or female, other than the ever present risk of an unwanted pregnancy, or perhaps a disease.

Legal
A common law marriage is a legally valid marriage which is entered without formalities or solemnization. There are no witnesses, license, exchanges of vows or promises before an authorized representative of the community (judge, pastor, etc.) or formal recording of the marriage in public records. Because marrying was long regarded as a natural right, one could marry without complying with legal formalities unless some statute required solemnization for validity.

Today about a quarter of the states recognize common law marriages if the parties have an intention to be married, cohabit as husband and wife, and hold themselves out to the community as husband and wife. Typically the validity of a common law marriage does not arise until a court must determine the question as part of determining some related claim, e.g. a claim for a spousal share of an estate, a claim for spousal benefits from a governmental agency such as the Social Security Administration, proof of marriage for purposes of filing a joint tax return, claims of bigamy (being married to more than one person at the same time), questions concerning the legitimacy of children, applicability of the spousal evidentiary privilege or intrafamily immunity in torts, or claims of creditors. When the issue is raised, it is the burden of the one claiming there was a marriage to prove the three requisites: intention to marry, cohabitation as husband and wife, and holding themselves out to the community as husband and wife. The latter is easiest if the couple adopt one name, take property as joint tenants, put joint names on accounts, and live in the community as husband and wife. It is more difficult where cohabitants expressly intend not to marry and deliberately avoid creating economic interdependence between themselves.

Since the requisite holding out as husband and wife must only be for what the court considers a reasonable time, unmarried couples who sojourn in one of the states which recognizes common law marriages may be found to have entered a common law marriage during a visit to such state. A short visit is not long enough, but vacations in the state have been found to be sufficient time.

Ethical

Judaic literature presents no concept at all of cohabitation or "living together," or the common law spouse. Islam historically has had a custom of mut'a, or temporary marriage. However, this custom, even among the fundamentalist Shiites is almost non-existent today. Buddhism does not have any such semi-marital custom or institution. Christianity has no religiously sanctioned or prohibited teachings regarding cohabitation.

Cohabitation, or living together, in the United States is widespread today, but is not dealt with by official religious teachings. The practice is prevalent among even the fundamentalist and charismatic communities. If it is spoken of at all in sermons it is usually referred to as "living in sin." However, pastoral counseling is the point of ethical and religious contact that the synagogues, churches, mosques, and temples make with persons living together without marriage.

Legal conflicts between persons who have lived together but are estranged from each other do occur, but apparently more commonly among the rich and famous. See 5 PALIMONY-LEGAL.

Psychological

Common law marriage, although acceptable to some, for many others lacks the commitment psychologically necessary for feelings of security and support. Feelings of insecurity and shame may be more predominant among females cohabiting without marriage, especially when children result.

7 PROMISCUITY

Medical

The medical risks involved in promiscuous sexual behavior, for the male or female, are the risks of disease or unwanted pregnancy.

Legal

A person who is sexually promiscuous may encounter a number of legal problems. Indiscriminate sexual contacts may run afoul of state statutes prohibiting certain types of sexual behavior, such as adultery (intercourse with a person who is married to another) or fornication (intercourse between unmarried persons). Promiscuity also increases the likelihood of contracting a venereal disease. A person who knows or has reason to know that he or she is infected with a venereal disease may be financially liable for transmitting that disease to an unsuspecting partner. Additionally, in many states a person who has sexual intercourse knowing that he or she is infected may be guilty of a crime.

Ethical

Promiscuity is condemned by Judaism, Islam, Buddhism, and Christianity. A common reason for condemning it is that sexual behavior with strangers is fraught with danger of disease. In Jewish teachings it is considered foolish, unwise, and wrongheaded. In Islam, it is considered whoremongering. In Buddhism, it diverts the person from the victory of nonattachment, of freedom from both craving and dejection. It is contrary to the Path of Right Mindfulness which involves control of body, mind, and feeling. It is a breach of the third of the Five Precepts: To abstain from sexual immorality. In Christianity, promiscuity is a sin against one's own body which is the temple of the Holy Spirit, and, if one is married it is adulterous behavior making the spouse vulnerable to disease. See 29 FORNICATION-ETHICAL.

Psychological

Promiscuity may, psychologically, be a symptom of a sociopath especially if accompanied by a lack of concern for the feelings of sexual partners and others.

Promiscuity may indicate a low level of self-esteem. For example, teenage girls feeling a need to gain acceptance among desired peers may become promiscuous to attract attention, and boys may attempt to prove their self-doubted virility by pursuing a loveless but active sex life.

Sexually abused girls are psychologically also at risk for becoming promiscuous.

The underlying mental conditions that promote promiscuity can often be treated. The confusion of physical attraction and emotional engagement are highly individualized psychological elements; such confusion can be evaluated only in terms of an individual's personal frame of reference.

8   SECURITY

Legal

It is alleged that homosexuals will not be given security clearances by the government because of their susceptibility to blackmail threats. There have also been some court cases concerning denial of security clearances or promotion or re-enlistment in the military to homosexuals. Normally if such issues come before a court, the result will be deference to national security interests and the express constitutional authority of the President as Commander-in-Chief over all decisions concerning military personnel and of the Congress as the body to declare war.

See 9 HOMOSEXUALITY–LEGAL

Psychological

Homosexuals are considered to be more vulnerable to blackmail than heterosexuals because in society there is still considerable lack of their acceptance. The personal contacts of a homosexual may not wish to be identified as acquaintances of the homosexual; the possibility of threats of exposure to acquaintances adds to the risk of blackmailing the homosexual.

9   HOMOSEXUALITY

Medical

Other than increased risk of disease and surface injuries from anal intercourse, there are no medical problems likely to result from male homosexual behavior. Classically, such behavior is interpreted as non-physiologic and not compatible with the physiologic life cycle or reproductive cycle; in this line of reasoning, homosexuality, if widely practiced, would lead to the depopulation of the species.

Sexually transmitted diseases that are more common among male homosexuals than among others include hepatitis B and AIDS.

The Medical Editors know of no significant medical problems arising from female homosexual behavior.

Legal

In criminal law the term "homosexuality" (or the female term "lesbianism") is not used.

In the common law, homosexuality was the crime "which should not even be named" and it was referred to as "the abomi-

nable and detestable crime against nature with man or beast."
That language is still found in the statutes of eight states. The
states which do criminalize homosexual acts usually do so under
a statute forbidding sodomy. Sodomy refers to sexual acts between two males and may or may not refer to acts between two
females. Many laws now include sodomy within a definition of
deviate sexual intercourse (sexual contact with the anus or mouth).
See 10 ORAL SEX; see also 11 ANAL SEX. The majority of states penalize such acts only if they are the result of force or the victim
does not consent, they are done in public, or the victim is below
the requisite age. See 25 STATUTORY RAPE.

In civil law stable homosexual relationships may be included
within statutory definitions of "family"—e.g., for purposes of a
rent control act or eligibility for public benefits.

No state allows same-sex marriages or the issuing of a marriage license to persons of the same sex, because the relationship
they enter is not what tradition has called marriage. If it is discovered after marriage that the parties are of the same sex, the
marriage may be declared invalid, often on the grounds of fraud.
A few recent cases have upheld marriages between spouses one
of whom has had sex-altering surgery and has adopted the corresponding sexual identity (gender).

In constitutional law the U.S. Supreme Court has determined (in *Bowers v. Hardwick*, 1986) that homosexual acts do not
fall within the zone of privacy recognized for contraception,
sterilization, abortion and child rearing; thus states remain constitutionally free to criminalize homosexual conduct. For the same
reason homosexuals do not fall within constitutional and statutory protections against discrimination and may experience discrimination in employment, housing, and public accommodations.
See 8 SECURITY.

Ethical

Jewish law condemns homosexuality as the practice of
idolaters. Leviticus 18:22 labels it as "an abomination." Josiah
"broke down the houses of male prostitutes which were in the
house of the Lord." (II Kings 23:7) In addition to being a form of
idolatry to the Jews, homosexuality was a waste of semen, an
unnatural act, an avoidance of the responsibilities of parenthood.

In Islam, the Koran describes homosexuality as "such an
indecency as never any being in all the world committed before
you." It then pronounces destruction upon the offenders. (Arberry
Translation, Vol. I, Ch. VII, line 73ff) The condemnation is repeated several times in the Koran.

In Buddhism, homosexuality would be a form of sexual misconduct, a breach of the third of the Five Precepts, that is: To abstain from sexual immorality, one can presume. However, Buddhism would have an essentially nonlegalistic and nonpunitive orientation. Typically, Buddha would say: "This beseems you," or "This does not beseem you."

In early Christian literature, homosexuality is also seen as idolatry in which the worship of the Creator is exchanged for the worship of the creature. (Romans 1:27 and I Corinthians 6:9) It is a misuse of the body. "The body is not meant for immorality but for the Lord, and the Lord for the body." (I Corinthians 6:12)

The Judaeo-Christian teachings since Biblical times have perpetuated the condemnation of homosexuality. The Vatican letter, "On the Pastoral Care of Homosexual Persons" issued in October, 1986, holds that those who find themselves homosexual must seek to change their orientation through prayer and counseling, or live totally chaste, celibate, sexually inactive lives. However, a book by John H. McNeill, a Catholic theologian, entitled *The Church and the Homosexual* (New York: Sheed, Andrews, and McMeel, 1976), interprets homosexuality in a much more positive way. He sees homosexual persons as having many gifts to bring to the life of the Church. He challenges the traditional view that God intends all human beings to be heterosexual, that anything other than heterosexuality is moral deviation and a sin or sickness.

A similarly vigorous debate is going on today in the mainline Protestant churches. Church leaders are discussing whether or not to ordain homosexual persons to their ministry. Fundamentalist churches, however, hold firmly to the traditional position, very much the same as that of the Vatican letter of October, 1986.

However, homosexual men and women have not waited for the established Christian churches to welcome them. They have organized a network of churches throughout the United States, called the Metropolitan Churches of America. They have their own ministers, literature, and Biblical interpretations.

Psychological

There is probably no culture in which homosexuality has not been reported.

In our society, homosexuality has become a highly charged emotional matter in many quarters; and the critics of homosexuals as well as the homosexuals themselves, have become the sub-ject of serious study in professional psychological circles.

Regarding the psychology of the critics of homosexuals, Gregory Herek, a psychologist at the University of California at Davis is reported (Daniel Goleman, "Studying Anti-Gay Bias", *The Courier Journal* [Louisville], July 23, 1990) to have said that for such critics, "Homosexuals stand as a proxy for all that is evil." He adds: "Some people see hating gay men and lesbians as a litmus test for being a moral person." Such persons often act out of adherence to religious beliefs that homosexuality is a sin. See ETHICAL, above.

Regarding the psychology of homosexuals: "Homosexual behavior is a complex phenomenon. In some people, it may be related to as yet undefined intrauterine hormonal influences (Note: They are born so. Psychological Editor). In these people, there appears to be a lifelong pattern of homosexual interests. For others, homosexual behavior appears to be related to psy-chological influences in the patient's early development, such as fear of heterosexual relationships.

"Homosexuality is not an illness, nor is it necessarily asso-ciated with 'femininity' in the male or 'masculinity' in the female. Homosexuals of both sexes share the same sexual concerns and problems of interpersonal relationships as heterosexuals. Homo-sexual relationship patterns can vary from extreme promiscuity to stable long-term relationships.

"Some people may seek medical or psychiatric help if they experience distress specifically from their homosexual concerns. These include adolescents with homosexual impulses who have not acted upon them or people who have been functioning homosexually but wish to function heterosexually. Others may be functioning heterosexually but have homosexual impulses, and still others may mistakenly develop fears of homosexuality because of sexual problems, such as loss of sexual desire or im-potence in a heterosexual setting.

"Many of these people need only simple reassurance. Oth-ers, however, should undergo therapy. In general, psychotherapy concentrates on dealing with the problems entailed in being ho-mosexual in a predominantly heterosexual society. Other patients may want to shift to a heterosexual orientation. About 1 out of 3 male homosexuals can be helped to shift his sexual orientation provided he still has had one or more successful heterosexual encounters, and he had his first homosexual experience after the age of 16." (The Columbia University College of Physicians and Surgeons, *Complete Home Medical Guide* [New York: Crown, 1985], 158)

Homosexuality has not been considered a mental illness in the U.S. since 1973; it was deleted from the American Psychiatric Association's *Diagnostic and Statistical Manual of Mental Disorders*, 3rd Ed. Revised (Washington, DC: American Psychiatric Association, 1987) (also known as DSM III) in 1975, and thereafter has been considered by most medical professionals to be an alternative sexual identity.

Homosexuality may cause individual feelings of discomfort and distress; therapy for the feelings should be sought in such cases. It is important to remember that sexuality is only one aspect of a person's life.

10 ORAL SEX

Medical

Infectious problems can arise from oral sex, for males and females, because of exposure to the variety of microorganisms present in and on the genital tract and in the mouth; infections of the throat or the mouth by microorganisms from the genitals, or infections of the genitals by microorganisms from the mouth, are not uncommon.

There is little that can be done to reduce the risk of such infections other than abstaining from oral sex. Avoiding genitalia that appear abnormal is an obvious precaution, but of course is not a reliable preventive of disease transmission. Thorough washing with soap and water both before and after contact reduces the amount of skin, genital, and fecal bacteria that may be transmitted.

Legal

Oral sex is sometimes included in legal definitions of sexual intercourse (any penetration however slight of any part of a person's body into another person's genital opening) or deviate sexual intercourse (any contact between the sex organs of one person and the mouth of another). Some jurisdictions now define the crime by specific reference to cunnilingus (oral stimulation of a female) or fellatio (oral stimulation of a male).

In over half of the states sexual acts are criminal only if performed by violence or against the will of the victim, if performed with a minor (see 25 STATUTORY RAPE), or if performed in public. In the other states oral sex may be a crime if the parties are not married to each other and, in a few states, even if they are married to each other.

Ethical

Specific teachings about oral sex, as such, are not spelled out in the sacred writings of Judaism, Islam, Buddhism, or Christianity. However, by inference, the practice would be condemned because it is "unnatural," by which is meant that it does not involve procreation or penile-vaginal intercourse. The teachings about masturbation would be applicable to oral sex, to some extent. See 3 MASTURBATION-ETHICAL.

However, in some fundamentalist churches oral sex by unmarried persons would be tolerated because it avoids violating the virginity of the couple whereas penile-vaginal intercourse would.

Psychological

Psychological problems need not be involved if both partners accept oral sexual activity; many dislike the idea of oral sex, believing it to be unhygienic, and medically risky. More women are negative about fellatio than about cunnilingus; and many find fellatio unacceptable, even abhorrent. Kinsey's studies indicated cunnilingus to be a common activity; nevertheless, many of both sexes still do not accept it.

Psychological problems of shame, anger, disgust, and communication occur when one partner desires oral sex when such is repugnant to the other.

11   ANAL SEX

Medical

In addition to the transmission of venereal disease, receptive anal intercourse can irritate the rectal area and sensitive anal membranes, leading to pain, discomfort, fissures, tears, and fecal bacterial infections.

Disease transmission by anal sex can be reduced by the use of a condom. Irritation may be minimized by use of a lubricant. The rectal canal, however, is much thinner walled and more easily ruptured than the healthy vagina which has such versatile musculature that it can contract, or dilate enough to permit the passage of a baby's head.

Legal

Anal sex is treated much as oral sex. See 10 ORAL SEX. Definitions of deviate sexual intercourse include any contact between the sex organs of one person and the anus of another.

In over half of the states such actions are not criminal unless there is physical force or lack of consent by the victim, the victim is under the legal age of consent (see 25 STATUTORY RAPE), or the act is in public. In other states it may be a crime if the parties are not married to each other and in a few states even if they are married to each other.

Ethical

In the Old Testament and the Talmud, Judaic law treats anal sex, also known as sodomy and buggery, as a serious sin. One reason for condemnation was that it was practiced widely by the Jews' pagan neighbors. Rehoboam, the son of Solomon, brought a cult of male prostitutes into the temple. (I Kings 14:24) Another reason for this condemnation was that it was "unnatural" and did not result in the birth of children, as is true of heterosexual intercourse.

In Islam, anal sex would be condemned because God did not create the anus to be used for sexual purposes. It is a misuse and an abuse of God's creation.

Buddhism's third of the Five Precepts: To abstain from sexual immorality, would be applicable to anal sex. "Right mindfulness" would include this precept in overcoming both the craving and despair common in the world. It would be a hindrance to "right concentration" which leads to Nirvana.

In Christianity, anal sex would be considered as a part of the behavior of a homosexual person, and would be disallowed on this basis. Christianity would be in keeping with Islam in that anal sex is a misuse and abuse of God's creation because the anus was not created to be used for sexual purposes. All the above applies between man and woman, as well as between man and man.

Psychological

Most psychologists believe that both homosexual and heterosexual consenting couples may perform anal intercourse without psychological problems, although such intercourse is far more frequent among homosexual males than among heterosexual couples. However, a heterosexual couple may develop problems of anger and communication when one partner desires anal sex and the other does not.

12   BESTIALITY

Medical

Bestiality, or sexual connection with an animal, offends the morality of individuals and fortunately cannot establish pregnancy. The medical reason for prohibiting bestiality is trauma to the genital tract and exposure to a variety of unusual bacteria which are likely to cause severe infections.

Legal

Bestiality is sexual contact between a human and an animal. In most states it is a criminal offense, under bestiality, offenses against morals, or cruelty to animal statutes. Punishments vary from modest fines and short prison terms to large fines and fairly significant prison terms.

The manufacture, distribution and sale of pornography that includes acts of bestiality is punished under obscenity laws.

Ethical

Judaism, Islam, Buddhism, and Christianity condemn bestiality.

CONDOMS

A condom is a tubular sheath fitted over the penis that serves to reduce the chance of venereal infection, or of conception, during sexual engagement. It is usually made of rubber or plastic, and in slang is often referred to as a *rubber* or *safe*. However, a skin condom, made from part of a lamb's large intestine, is also manufactured.

The condom—and only the condom—acts as a barrier against the transmission of a disease between sexual partners; and also as a contraceptive, blocking the passage of sperm into the vagina to avoid conception. Condoms are readily available almost everywhere without a prescription at a relatively low cost, or sometimes at no cost. Because of these facts, the use of condoms is widely recommended. See 13 CONDOMS.

Risks

The use of a condom, which is the only birth control and disease prevention device available for use by a male, is not always effective. Careless use, or a tear (see 14 CONDOMS vs. ANAL OR ORAL SEX), or even a small hole in a defective one, sometimes defeats its mission as a prophylactic and/or as a contraceptive. See 15 USE.

Considerations

The chances of transmitting or contracting a disease or of creating an unwanted pregnancy from a casual sexual encounter, if a good quality condom is properly used, seem to be relatively small; but the gain versus the chance of loss should be considered.

The gain would be the satisfaction of the sexual encounter, but the loss would be creating an unwanted pregnancy, or of transmitting or contracting a debilitating, or even deadly, disease. While the chance of such loss might be small statistically, nevertheless some persons will consider a casual encounter a high-risk venture with the penalty far too severe to be worth any risk at all for what might be considered a relatively small gain.

The female has more at risk than the male from a casual sexual encounter. While both can suffer, it is she who usually suffers more than the male from a venereal disease and/or an unwanted pregnancy.

---

13   CONDOMS

Medical

For condom users, latex condoms are strongly advised because of their relative reliability and consistency of manufacture. The user should inspect the condom prior to its application to determine whether tears or holes are present. Care should be taken to avoid tearing the condom with a fingernail. Prelubricated condoms are desirable as well as condoms with a variety of latex attachments to the tip.

There are no negative medical consequences likely to affect males or females by the use of condoms, unless one of the partners is allergic to latex which irritates the genital area.

Today condoms may be bought in many commonly frequented locations, including drug stores and supermarkets, service stations, night clubs, and restaurants.

In March, 1989, a *Consumer Reports* study entitled "Can You Rely on Condoms?" was published. The study reports the results of laboratory tests intended to determine which brands are most likely to protect against sexually transmitted disease. Reprints are available in bulk from: CU/Reprints, P. O. Box CS 2010-A, Mount Vernon, NEW YORK 10551.

Legal

Engaging in sexual intercourse when a person knows or has reason to know that he or she is infected with a venereal disease is a crime in many states. This is so even if the person has taken precautions against transmitting that disease by using a condom. Likewise, use of a condom may not be a defense to a claim that a person negligently transmitted a venereal disease to his or her unsuspecting partner in a civil suit for damages. See 19 DAMAGES.

Ethical

The only explicit teaching about the use of condoms in Judaism, Islam, Buddhism, or Christianity is the modern Roman Catholic rule against artificial contraception of any kind. This Catholic rule has had extensive cultural impact on the unspoken resistance to teaching sex education in general and contraception in particular.

The attitudes of conservative Protestants are sometimes indistinguishable from Catholic teachings.

Even in liberal religious traditions a remarkable silence about condoms and the AIDS epidemic prevails. The "hush hush" stance has the effect of moral condemnation. The neglect of teachings about sex in the churches makes the use of condoms a part of the larger issue, namely inability and unwillingness to deal with the sex education of youth.

Psychological

Sexual intercourse with a condom has often been described by males as "like washing your foot with your sock on" indicating dissatisfaction with the loss of tactile sensation; such loss may be balanced by feelings of relative safety. For most males, the use of a condom will not produce psychological problems. If such do arise, they are likely to be superficial and temporary.

Condom failure may produce feelings of guilt, betrayal, negligence, or frustration.

Excuses given for not using condoms include embarrassment from discussing and effecting their use in the presence of a partner; or in being seen while purchasing them; or a loss of spontaneity; or because the male wishes to make the female responsible for avoiding an unwanted pregnancy.

Some females are uncomfortable with intercourse for enjoyment rather than for reproduction. These feelings may be especially acute when intercourse is practiced with a condom, which reinforces these feelings by interrupting the spontaneity of love-making. Other females may be more able to enjoy intercourse if their fears and anxieties about infection or unwanted pregnancy are lessened by the use of a condom.

14 CONDOMS vs. ANAL OR ORAL SEX

Medical

Lubricated latex condoms are recommended for those who engage in anal sex, to reduce the risk of infection or disease transmission and the consequences of abrasion.

"Adolescents should be instructed about 'safe sex' which may require description or at least mention of practices such as anal intercourse which increase the risk of serious infection or injuries." (King K. Holmes, et al., *Sexually Transmitted Diseases*, 2nd ed., [New York: McGraw-Hill, 1990], 82)

For those who engage in oral sex, there are no prophylactic devices, pills, salves, ointments, or the like to reduce the risk of disease transmission; it is doubtful that condoms can be used effectively in the practice of such sex. Thorough washing with soap and water, as well as showering, reduces the likelihood of infection.

Legal

See 13 CONDOMS, 10 ORAL SEX, and 11 ANAL SEX.

Psychological

Using condoms during anal sex as a safety measure in preventing the transmission of common infections or venereal disease should normally present no psychological problems.

See MEDICAL, above.

15 USE

Medical

For those who rely on the condom to reduce the risk of disease and unwanted pregnancy, its use in every instance of sexual intercourse and anal sex is imperative.

After the condom has been inspected for defects and applied, a lubricant such as surgical jelly, which is available in drug stores without prescription, is recommended if the condom is not prelubricated; however, if a latex condom is used, lubricants which might weaken the condom, namely, oil-based lubricants such as mineral oil and petroleum jelly, should be avoided. See 13 CONDOMS-MEDICAL.

SOCIAL DISEASES*

Commonly called "VDs." However, in the medical profession, and among disease research professionals, venereal diseases are increasingly being referred to as "sexually transmitted diseases," or "STDs."

*"Social disease, a disease ordinarily spread by social contact, esp. a venereal disease." *The Random House College Dictionary*, Revised Edition, (New York: Random House, 1988)

CONTROLLING STDs

Public Health

For the benefit of its citizens, the United States has a well developed public health disease control system. STDs are included in this system.

One of the objectives of the system is to insure, as far as possible, that all STD transmitters and those they put at risk are medically treated. This objective is pursued by the collection, analysis, and dissemination of information; and by the discovery, diagnosis, and treatment of infected persons.

The initial case discovery and reporting responsibilities are with private physicians, hospitals, and clinics nationwide. These three front-line units are required by state laws to report to county health departments cases of designated STDs and other diseases.

The information reported is confidential.

Details vary from state to state, but are complete as to the disease and the location of the infected individual. If the risk to the diseased person and/or to his or her sexual partner or partners is sufficiently high, public health action is taken for their protection.

Each week, county health departments relay case data to state health departments for review and collation. A state health department, for example, makes certain that a disease diagnosis in County A of a County B resident reaches the County B health department. Likewise, a State X health department makes certain that a disease diagnosis in State X of a State Y resident reaches the State Y health department. Some states publish monthly newsletters summarizing their data.

43

Weekly, the states send case data to the Centers for Disease Control (CDC), a federal agency, located in Atlanta. One of CDC's publications is the *Morbidity and Mortality Weekly Report* which presents disease data and has articles on current medical topics.

From this CDC system come data useful in defining patterns of disease occurrence and in planning country-wide prevention and control programs. Besides checking the treatment and cure of local individuals, county health departments cooperate in such national programs.

There are some inconsistencies. For example, one state uses a single card to report diseases; another uses three. One state identifies 68 reportable diseases; another, 45. The only STDs that are reported consistently by all states are AIDS, syphilis, and gonorrhea.

Inconsistencies notwithstanding, the overall system is important to the individual's and the nation's health; and individual cooperation with the system is highly important.

Education's Role

"Adolescent reproductive health care is best served by prevention of biopsychosocial consequences. Many adults believe that adolescents should refrain from sexual intercourse until marriage or at least until they have a mature committed relationship in which both partners are able and willing to take responsibility for any consequences. Many professionals believe that first intercourse should be postponed at least until the reproductive system is fully mature (late teens) and until there is sufficient psychosocial maturity for responsible behavior. If adolescents are willing to postpone first coitus, they remain at risk for transmission of STDs through noncoital intimate behaviors; however, it may by unrealistic to expect adolescents to abstain from all physical expressions of sexuality, especially if marriage is unlikely until the middle or late twenties.

"Adolescents who will not be persuaded to abstain from intercourse must be well informed about the risks of all forms of sexual intimacy and provided with the knowledge and methods for prevention of infection and pregnancy. Teenagers should be encouraged to use barrier contraceptives, especially both condom and vaginal spermicide, with every coital act, whether or not the female is using the oral contraceptive. Adolescents should be instructed about 'safe sex' which may require description or at least mention of practices such as anal intercourse which increase the risk of serious infections or injuries. Sexually active teenagers, even those consistently using barrier methods and having a single partner, should be screened yearly for infections. More frequent screening should be considered for high-risk adolescents such as gay youths, runaways, drug abusers, and delinquents.

"Sex education or family life education does not guarantee prevention of consequences, will not ensure abstinence, and has not been shown to increase sexual experimentation. Teenagers who have been exposed to appropriate sex education tend to delay first intercourse, to use contraception when then have intercourse, and to avoid pregnancy. Family life education of children and adolescents is a responsibility shared by parents, schools, health professionals, and other adults who provide services to youth. All contribute positively or negatively to each young person's understanding about and attitude toward human sexuality. Parents and other family members begin this process at childbirth and provide the major influence in the development of personal values and beliefs. Society's unresolved debate about the content and timing of sexuality education and parental reluctance to discuss sexuality topics often leave youth uninformed or misinformed. Incomplete or inaccurate sexual information tends to be derived from friends, the media, and available written materials ranging from dictionaries to sex-oriented adult magazines.

"As children reach adolescence, the normal distancing from parents may interfere with open communication and effective education even in the most enlightened and comfortable families. Health professionals can be important allies of parents and schools in providing scientific information and the latest technical advances, in supporting developmentally appropriate communication within families, and in helping the community accept the importance of lifelong comprehensive family life education for all families. Professionals can be available to assist individual parents in educating their children and themselves and to assist in planning and promoting family life education curricula and opportunities in schools, churches, and other community settings." (King K. Holmes, et al., *Sexually Transmitted Diseases*, 2nd ed., [New York: McGraw-Hill, 1990], 82)

Courses in sexuality are taught in many high schools and colleges.   One college-level text book that is comprehensive and clear is *Understanding Human Sexuality*, Third Edition, by Janet Sibley Hyde (New York: McGraw Hill, 1986).

Where One May Call For Guidance

The U.S. National STD Hotline number for information is 1-800-227-8922. It is toll-free, and open from 8:00 AM until 11:00 PM, Eastern Time, Monday through Friday.

The U.S. National AIDS Hotline number is 1-800-342-AIDS. It is toll-free, and open 24 hours daily, seven days per week.

In 1987 about 58,000 calls in the U.S. on the STD hotline were answered; over 30,000 asked for referral to confidential medical services.

In the last three months of the same year, the AIDS taped message hotline averaged 50,000 calls a month; 20,000 callers a month asked for operator service after listening to the tape.

CONSEQUENCES OF TRANSMISSION

Venereal or social diseases have long been regarded as loathsome; most must be taken very seriously. See 16 PROSTITUTION. A few are easily cured and are primarily worrisome. See 17 DIAGNOSIS. Others can be debilitating and even deadly to the infected, and crippling to an offspring. Some, if untreated in females, can cause ectopic pregnancies or infertility. Some can be treated (see 18 TREATMENT) for relatively few dollars; others must be treated at great expense in dollars and time.

The transmission of most venereal diseases is not to be treated lightly. If the transmission is deliberate, or even if it results from carelessness or is simply accidental, there may be injury which could result in serious consequences for both parties (the wrongdoer who transmits the disease and the victim who receives it).

Insurance companies are increasingly wary of communicable disease insurance. One company recently stated: the "...transmission of communicable diseases, and lawsuits alleging such transmission, have begun to appear with greater frequency." See 19 DAMAGES. The company now provides no coverage under the Homeowners policy for injury arising out of the transmission of a communicable disease by an insured. See 20 HEALTH INSURANCE.

Thus a transmitter may become a target without an insurance shield against law suits.

However, the legal jeopardy may be the least of the transmitter's worries; the moral and psychological effects from a guilty conscience (see 21 GUILT) may persist long

47

after the financial hazard may have evaporated. The degree of guilt may vary depending upon the relationship of the injured to the transmitter. If the injury is to a loved one, such as a wife perhaps, or a husband, the degree of guilt of the transmitter can be especially traumatic and haunting for years.

---

16   PROSTITUTION

Medical

Contrary to the claims of some brothels, a periodic medical check of male and female prostitutes is not effective in preventing the transmission of venereal disease because of the frequency of their sexual activity relative to the frequency of inspection; and because of the relatively short incubation periods of most STDs.

For males who risk patronizing female prostitutes for sexual intercourse, the best method of trying to prevent disease is the use of condoms; for some additional protection, the prostitute may use a vaginal jelly which is spermicidal as well as antiviral.

However, patronizing prostitutes, male or female, remains medically a high risk, not only for prostitute and client, but also for other sexual partners.

Legal

It is rare to find a society where traditional prostitution is not subject to some type of legal regulation. In many western European nations, although prostitution involving adults is not a crime, many activities incidental to prostitution, such as procuring, pandering, pimping, and running a brothel may be criminal acts. Additionally, traditional street prostitution is often regulated using public nuisance and disorderly conduct laws. In some countries, the operation of a brothel may be legal, although subject to licensing by federal and local governments. Legal brothels usually can only be located in designated areas and prostitutes operating from these brothels must undergo regular physical examinations to detect venereal disease.

The United States remains one of the few western nations where the criminalization of prostitution is widespread. The notable exception is the State of Nevada, where the operation of a brothel may be legalized on a local option basis.

State prostitution laws vary in how criminal acts are defined and in how they are punished. Generally, prostitution itself is treated as a misdemeanor (involving fines or very short prison sentences), whereas pandering (enticing an individual to become a prostitute) or operating a brothel may be treated more seriously. Additionally, prostitution activities involving juveniles are considered the most serious of all prostitution crimes and can result in very long prison sentences.

States and localities also vary as to enforcement of prostitution laws. Enforcement, particularly in large urban areas, is often lax. Clients of prostitutes frequently are not charged with crimes, even if their association with prostitutes constitutes a criminal act.

There is a trend toward treating prostitution as a public nuisance or violation of public indecency or obscenity laws. There is and has been for some time a strong advocacy in this country for decriminalizing and even licensing adult prostitution. Many argue that prostitution is a "victimless" crime, and therefore, should be treated as a private and legal contractual arrangement between consenting participants. Conversely, some argue that the primary victims of prostitution are the prostitutes themselves. There is particular concern over the exploitation of prostitutes by organized crime establishments. Some reason, therefore, that legalization and licensing of prostitution would enable the state to protect men and women engaged in selling sexual favors from exploitation by third parties. Lastly, it is argued that the spread of venereal diseases can better be controlled by requiring prostitutes to submit to regular medical examinations as a condition for maintaining their trade license; such control, however, is far from medical certainty.

Ethical

Judaism rejects prostitution. The Old Testament relates it to the prostitution cults, both male and female, that were practiced by non-Jewish neighbors. In Islam, the Sales translation of the Koran says: "If any of your women be guilty of whoredom (which includes both adultery and fornication) produce four witnesses from you against them, and if they bear witness, then detain them in houses until death releases them or God appoints for them a way."

Buddhism, in its Eightfold Path to Nirvana, would consider prostitution a breach of the fourth step, Right Action, which requires that one refrain from conduct in matters of bodily pleasure (especially wrongful sexual practices of which prostitution would be one). In Buddhism, the Third Precept (To abstain from sexual immorality) forbids fornication with kept women, women bought with money, women bought by the gift of a garment, concubines, girls captured in war, and temporary wives. (Edward Conze, selector and translator, *Buddhist Scriptures* [London: Penguin Books, 1939], 71)

Christianity rejects prostitution on the assumption and in the belief that the sexual act makes "one flesh" of a couple. The Apostle Paul says, "Do you not know that he who joins himself to a prostitute becomes one body with her flesh? For it is written, 'The two shall become one flesh.'" (I Corinthians 6:16) However, in the ministry of Jesus, he recognized that a woman prostitute was a sinner, but he treated her with great compassion. He expressed his gratitude for her anointing his feet with ointment. He said: "Her sins are forgiven for she has loved much ..." (Luke 7:36-50, esp. 47)

Prostitution involves both men and women. The social ethic of Judaism, Islam Buddhism, and Christianity considers more than merely a person's behavior. All four consider the organized crime aspect of prostitution traffic, and the responsibility of the man who participates as well as that of the woman. Then, too, the uncleanliness and the spread of sexually transmitted diseases is another concern of religious, social ethics.

Psychological

Female prostitutes often suffer guilt, loss of self-esteem, and hostility towards men. Aging prostitutes are increasingly vulnerable to depression, anxiety, and substance abuse.

Male prostitutes are at risk for loss of self-esteem, shame, feelings of degradation, anxiety, depression, and substance abuse.

Male clients of female prostitutes frequently lack self confidence; have attitudes associating sex with sin; or may actually dislike women; others, suffering from sexual behavior problems (e.g., sexual masochism and sexual sadism) and lacking consenting partners, may purchase the services of prostitutes to act out their fantasies.

17 DIAGNOSIS

Medical

The early diagnosis of a venereal infection is imperative so that therapy is undertaken before permanent damage is done to the genital tract of the newly infected, and so that the transmitter may also be treated and cautioned about further transmission.

Psychological

A person newly diagnosed as having an STD often suffers feelings of regret, shame, guilt, isolation, the sense of being punished, and a fear of castigation for wrong-doing. If such feelings are suspected, the diagnosing physician should encourage psychological therapy. Furthermore, the physician should take care not to bring about such feelings because the person might avoid treating the disease to avoid having to endure the feelings.

18   TREATMENT

Medical

Some venereal diseases, such as gonorrhea, chlamydial infections, and chancroid, can be cured by treatment with a single course of antibiotics. The expense involves an initial office visit for diagnosis, laboratory tests for confirming the diagnosis, therapy, and and a follow-up office visit with a repeat laboratory test for proof of cure. Such treatment may cost between $75 and $150 if given by a private physician. On the other hand, treatment for genital herpes involves the same initial office visit, diagnosis, laboratory tests, and therapy, for about the same cost; however, because of recurrence, continuing visits to the physician and continuing medication, such as acyclovir, are necessary and cost approximately $50 to $60 more for each treatment. Treatment for AIDS is an extreme high example of cost in time and money. Self-diagnosis and treatment for pubic lice, on the other hand, is an extreme low example of such cost.

Treatments are usually not painful, beyond the minor pain of an injection.

19   DAMAGES

Legal

A person who knows or has reason to know that he or she is infected with a venereal disease may be found liable in a civil law suit for transmitting that disease to an unsuspecting sexual partner.

Liability for transmission of a venereal disease may also extend to non-partners of the defendant (for instance, the plaintiff's spouse) who were foreseeable victims of the defendant's conduct.

Given the serious and even life threatening nature of some venereal diseases, the potential for plaintiff's recovering very large financial settlements is high. A plaintiff who alleges to have been infected by a partner may pursue damages under a simple negligence theory, claiming that the defendant breached a duty to exercise ordinary care to avoid transmitting the disease. A defendant may be found negligent even if not aware of suffering from a venereal disease, provided that he or she had reason to know or suspect that he or she might be infected.

A plaintiff may also pursue legal claims based upon allegations that a defendant's harmful conduct was intentional, and not simply careless. To succeed under these theories, a plaintiff must demonstrate that the defendant actually knew of the infection, although he or she need not have known the exact nature of the disease.

Intentional torts or wrongs include actions for battery, fraudulent misrepresentation of the state of one's health and intentional infliction of emotional distress. The later theory is particularly useful for plaintiffs who are aggrieved because they have been exposed to the AIDS virus. In some states, a person may be able to recover damages to compensate for the fear and trauma caused simply by the possibility of developing the disease in the future.

Plaintiffs seeking financial damages from sexual partners may encounter a number of difficulties in pursuing their claims. If a plaintiff has a past history of promiscuity or high risk behavior, he or she may encounter difficulty in proving that it was the named defendant who transmitted the disease. This is a particular problem with claims arising from exposure to or infection with the HIV virus. A plaintiff's knowledge that defendant was infected with a venereal disease will defeat the claim because he or she will be found to have consented to the exposure. However, consent to have sexual relations is not held to be consent to disease exposure. Likewise, a defendant may claim that the plaintiff assumed the risk of exposure to the disease; or that the plaintiff was negligent for failing to protect himself or herself from infection, particularly if defendant's high risk sexual activity, and therefore the likelihood that he or she was infected, was known.

However, a plaintiff's assumption of the risk or negligence is never a defense to an intentional tort claim. If a defendant's actions have been particularly outrageous and offensive to common standards of decency, as is often alleged to be the case with intentional tort claims, the defendant may be assessed punitive damages. This type of damages was awarded to Marc Christian in his highly publicized suit against the estate of actor Rock Hudson, and Hudson's personal secretary. The jury found that the defendants concealed from Christian the fact that Hudson suffered from AIDS so that Christian would continue in his relationship with Hudson. Although Christian did not contract AIDS and consistently tested HIV-negative during the trial, he was awarded a multimillion dollar verdict, including punitive damages, because of the emotional distress caused by defendants' less than honest behavior.

It is important to note that in many states a person who engages in sexual activities while infected with a venereal disease may also incur criminal penalties. There is a possibility that a defendant who exposed a victim to the HIV virus during the commission of a crime (e.g., assault or rape) may be charged with attempted homicide or homicide.

Also, health care professionals who fail to warn partners of infected patients may be liable if the disease is transmitted to the unsuspecting partner. In some states, however, health care professionals may be prohibited by law from revealing to other persons the fact of a person's HIV infection. Furthermore, when the disease is not reportable by statute, as in the cases of molluscum and genital warts, for example, such warnings breach physician-patient confidentiality.

Ethical
If a person knowingly transmits a venereal disease to another, this would be viewed by all United States religious groups as a breach of responsible conduct. However, the affixing of guilt and the meting out of punishment would be a matter for courts to decide.

Psychological
The psychological "damages" to the transmitter of an STD can be severe. See 21 GUILT.

20   HEALTH INSURANCE
Medical
Typical health insurance policies can cover the expense of medically treating sexually transmitted diseases; often, however,

these policies do not cover the treatment cost if the disease existed when insurance coverage began. Policies may contain specific limitations on treating the emotional or psychiatric elements of a disease, such as depression, anxiety, and the like.

Legal

A health insurance policy generally does not cover conditions from which the insured suffered on the date the policy became effective. Additionally, insurance may not cover treatment for certain complications of venereal diseases such as infertility.

Obtaining and keeping health insurance coverage may be difficult for those who suffer from or are at risk of contracting serious and costly diseases such as AIDS. In most states, insurance companies have the right to obtain information about the health and the health risks of an applicant for an insurance policy, including the results of an HIV test. Even AIDS victims who have insurance may find that coverage is inadequate, because the costs of experimental or alternative treatment programs frequently are not reimbursed. Although some states have adopted laws that make private health insurance plans accessible to high risk persons, as a rule, obtaining adequate health insurance will remain a crisis for AIDS victims.

21   GUILT

Ethical

Judaism has an elaborate system of law by which innocence or guilt is decided. The law is taught to Jewish children both in the family and in the synagogues. It is dramatized in impressive rituals on high holy days and in family rituals, daily. The "Thou Shalts ..." and the "Thou Shalt Nots ..." become a part of the fabric of the consciousness of Jewish children. The system of law is the source of guilt or innocence that guides, or weighs down, the Jewish person.

Islam builds a similar guilt-innocence structure into the lives of adherents by means of intensive daily prayers. The reading of the Koran and the rituals of the home induce an effect similar to that found in Judaism.

Buddhism is far less moralistic and legalistic. The emphasis is upon "seemly" and "unseemly" behavior. More attention is given to appropriate and inappropriate behavior. The emphasis seems not to be so much upon inducing guilt, as upon inducing inspiration to follow the Eightfold Path.

Christianity varies from group to group on the matter of inducing guilt in followers.

The precepts of the Catholic Church are taught in the home and the parochial school. Contrary to liberal Protestantism, there is no hesitancy in church and school to teach the Catholic version of sexual morality to children. Protestant fundamentalist groups follow much the same approach as to content of teachings.

In liberal Catholic and Protestant groups, guilt is not used as a force. Instead, spiritual direction and pastoral care are used in small groups to inspire lives of sexual intimacy that fulfill the purposes of God, for the life of the marriage.

Psychological

Any person with a normal conscience will suffer guilt from either the knowing or the unknowing ("I should have known.") transmission of an STD. However, it is possible that a sociopath would knowingly pass an STD as a form of revenge or punishment, and feel pleasure, not guilt, for such an act.

The American Medical Association's *Encyclopedia of Medicine* (New York: Random House, 1989), on page 501, defines guilt as: "A painful feeling that arises from the awareness of having broken a moral or legal code. Guilt is self-inflicted, unlike shame, which depends on others knowing about the transgression. Some psychoanalysts see guilt as a result of the prohibitions of the superego (conscience) instilled by parental authority in early life. Others see guilt as a conditioned response to actions that in the past have led to punishment.

"Feeling guilty from time to time is normal. However, feeling very guilty for no reason or experiencing guilt at an imagined crime is one of the main symptoms of psychotic depression."

CHANCROID

Sometimes called *soft chancre*
(pronounced "shanker"), or *soft sore.*

Who's Affected

Males and females alike can be infected, although in the late 1980's over five males were reported infected for every female infected.

Cause

Chancroid (an infectious venereal ulcer) is an infection by the bacterium Haemophilus ducreyi.

Symptoms

The symptoms of chancroid in both males and females are, characteristically, painful genital ulcers and, in about one half the cases, painfully enlarged lymph nodes in the groin. The ulcers begin as chancres, which are tender pimple-like sores, and in 24 to 48 hours they become eroded, open, and pustular. See SYPHILIS-SYMPTOMS, page 71; also see GENITAL HERPES-SYMPTOMS, page 86.

About half the males affected will have one ulcer; the other half will have many. Usually ulcers are located on or near the foreskin of the penis; swelling of the foreskin is common. Less frequently, the glans or the shaft of the penis may be affected.

In females, ulcers usually appear at the vaginal entrance; or between the vagina and rectum; or on the labia or clitoris. Large ulcers around the urethral opening are not uncommon; vaginal wall ulcers can also occur.

Diagnosis

Chancroid is initially diagnosed by its signs and symptoms, notably painful ulcers on the genitals and swollen lymph glands in the groin. However, in order to identify chancroid ulcers, as opposed to the ulcers of genital herpes or syphilis, laboratory tests, including bacterial cultures, are dictated.

Treatment

Chancroid is treated with antibiotics, usually erythromycin, taken orally over seven to ten days, or ceftriaxone, injected in a single dose. After treatment, the ulcers usually show improvement in three days and are cured after seven days.

Enlarged lymph glands are sometimes slower to heal; and treatment may require aspiration, that is, removal of fluid by needle.

Partner

When a person is diagnosed as having chancroid, any sexual partner within the ten days before the onset of symptoms must be informed of the diagnosis and promptly treated just the same as the infected person.

Rather than risk a condom shield, the infected person should not engage in sexual activity until at least ten days from the start of treatment have passed and there is no culture evidence of chancroid.

Once the infected person is cured, partner protection is not needed.

Follow-up

The patient should be observed until the ulcers are completely healed, lymph gland swelling has subsided, and bacterial cultures are negative.

A chancroid infected person should also be tested for syphilis, AIDS, and genital herpes.

Risks

If untreated, chancroid can cause painful, extensive tissue destruction with abscess formation in the groin. There, inflamed lymph glands can become bubos, which may rupture allowing pus to pass into the groin area.

Untreated chancroid becomes a protracted illness with slow and often incomplete resolution.

Outside the United States, chancroid has become associated with the spread of AIDS.

Incapacitation

An individual with chancroid may become physically incapacitated because of the pain from open lesions and swollen glands.

Transmission

Chancroid is transmitted by intimate contact, including sexual intercourse and possibly including oral and anal sex.

Avoidance

The use of a condom during sexual engagement reduces the risk of contracting or transmitting chancroid, but does not eliminate such risk. If a male has ulcers on the shaft of his penis, then a condom, if it covers the ulcers, will reduce the risk of infecting the female. If a female has ulcers on her labia, then a condom may reduce the risk of infecting the male. See SYMPTOMS, above.

There are no douches, salves, pills or the like to prevent the transmission of chancroid.

Incidence

In 1989, only 4,700 cases of chancroid were reported in the U.S. to the Centers for Disease Control. Historically, occurrences have mostly involved sailors and travellers who patronized prostitutes in the tropics. However, from 1985 to 1989, the number of reported chancroid cases more than doubled; and because the disease may enhance the transmission of AIDS, increasing attention is being paid to it.

CHLAMYDIAL INFECTIONS

Sometimes specifically striking as *epididymitis* and *prostatitis* in males; and *cervicitis, endometritis,* and *salpingitis,* which are often grouped as *pelvic inflammatory disease (PID),* in females. *Urethritis* and *rectal infection (proctitis)* occur in both sexes.

Who's Affected

Males and females without regard to age can be infected.

A baby born to a mother with chlamydial cervicitis may acquire conjunctivitis or pneumonia at delivery.

Cause

Chlamydial infections are caused by the Chlamydia trachomatis bacterium.

Symptoms

When a chlamydial infection is in the urethra, male or female, it is called urethritis, and the symptoms are pain upon urination and a watery, mucous discharge; the discharge is without pus.

When the infection spreads upward in the male, it may become epididymitis, or prostatitis. The symptoms of epididymitis are severe pain and a swollen testicle; and in acute cases, redness of the scrotum. The symptoms of prostatitis are pain upon urination, frequent urination, and sometimes blood in the urine; symptoms may also include fever and discharge from the penis.

When the infection spreads upward in the female, it may include cervicitis, endometritis, and salpingitis. The symptoms can be abdominal pain, vaginal discharge, and fever.

When the infection is in the rectum, male or female, it is called proctitis, and the symptoms are rectal bleeding, severe soreness, swelling of lymph nodes in the pelvic area, fever, a general feeling of ill health, and pain on defecation.

Often males and usually females will have no symptoms, but can still pass the infection on to sexual partners.

See GONORRHEA-SYMPTOMS, page 63; also see NONSPECIFIC URETHRITIS-SYMPTOMS, page 68.

Diagnosis

Diagnosis may be by laboratory culture.

In addition to difficult and expensive diagnosis by culture, there are three types of chlamydial screening tests currently in use and their sensitivity approaches that of chlamydial culture.

The cost is approximately $20 for a screening test.

Usually a screening test can be accomplished within several hours by the laboratory; however, it takes approximately two days to get the material to be tested to the laboratory, to have the laboratory run the test, and to have the results back to the physician.

Treatment

Chlamydial infections generally respond to the prescription antibiotics tetracycline or doxycycline, taken orally over ten to fourteen days. These drugs are photosensitizing and the patient should remain out of direct sunlight while being treated.

If the patient develops abdominal pain, fever, and increased white blood count, hospitalization for treatment with intravenous antibiotics may become necessary.

Successful treatment of chlamydial infection does not prevent re-infection.

Partner

When a person is diagnosed as having a chlamydial infection, any partner within the last 30 days must be informed of the diagnosis and promptly treated just the same as the infected person.

Since treatment of the infected person lasts ten to 14 days, and since it is not known at what point during these days the person becomes incapable of transmitting the disease, any sexual partner during the treatment period should be protected by abstinence, or at least by use of a condom.

At the end of treatment, the infected person is presumed cured; but treatment failures are possible; so, until a test-of-cure shows that a cure has been effected, any sexual partner should be protected by use of a condom. See FOLLOW UP, below.

Once the infected person is cured, partner protection is not needed.

Follow-up

When taken as directed, the prescription drugs have a 95% cure rate. However, a test-of-cure takes from three to six weeks after treatment; and when the test shows the treatment has not been effective, the patient should be re-treated.

A person who is diagnosed as having a chlamydial infection should also be tested for gonorrhea, syphilis, AIDS, and hepatitis B.

Risks

Untreated chlamydial infections in the male can lead to severe and chronic urethritis and in turn to stricture or obstruction of the urethra.

Untreated chlamydial infections in the female can lead to development of upper tract genital disease called pelvic inflammatory disease (PID). PID can lead to ectopic pregnancy, pelvic abscesses, chronic pelvic pain, or to infertility due to scarred or obstructed Fallopian tubes.

In both sexes, an untreated chlamydial rectal infection can lead to serious, chronic complications in the lower bowel with scarring and strictures.

Trachoma (chlamydial infection of the eye) can affect both sexes; untreated trachoma can lead to blindness.

See GONORRHEA-RISKS, page 65; also see NONSPECIFIC URETHRITIS-RISKS, page 69.

Incapacitation

Pain, and/or difficulty in urinating because of urethra occlusion, can be so severe as to be be physically incapacitating.

Transmission

Chlamydial infections are transmitted by direct contact with infected secretions, by sexual intercourse, by commonly used towels, and by anal sex.

Chlamydiae are organisms that live within cells, and the infectious material transmitted consists of cells from the infected person. If a person comes in contact with secretions containing intracellular chlamydiae, for example on unwashed hands or commonly used towels, and if the material is still near body temperature, it is possible for transmission to occur; if the secretions are below body temperature at room temperature, the intracellular chlamydiae are unlikely to be infectious.

Avoidance

The use of a condom in sexual engagement reduces the risk of contracting or transmitting chlamydial infections, for both males and females, but does not eliminate such risk.

There are no douches, salves, pills or the like to prevent the transmission of chlamydiae, but thorough washing and irrigation reduce the risk.

Incidence

The estimate of chlamydial infection; in the Unites States by the Centers for Disease Control is 3 to 4 million new cases a year.

For males, chlamydial infection causes about half of the reported cases of nongonococcal urethritis and epididymitis; for females it is the major cause of acute salpingitis.

It is estimated that in the U.S. from 5 to 13 percent of all females have chlamydial cervicitis now, frequently without symptoms.

GONORRHEA

Sometimes called *clap, strain, gleet, dose, drip, the whites,* GC.

Who's Affected

Males and females alike can be infected, especially those between the ages of 20 and 30 who have multiple sex partners. About one third more males than females contract gonorrhea.

The disease may be transmitted during delivery to a newborn by an infected mother and result in a severe inflammation in one or both of the newborn's eyes, which in some cases leads to blindness.

Cause

Gonorrhea is an infection caused by the long familiar Neisseria gonorrhoeae bacterium.

Symptoms

In males, the bacteria usually infect the urethra initially. In females, they usually infect the cervix at first. Cases of anal, oral, and ocular infection in both sexes are also known.

Symptoms appear between two and ten days after exposure. In males, symptoms are burning and pain in the urethra during urination, and the discharge of a yellowish, pus-like liquid from the urethra. Stains may appear on underwear.

In females, symptoms are a cloudy vaginal discharge, discomfort in the lower abdomen; a burning sensation while urinating; and/or abnormal (non-menstrual) vaginal bleeding. Stains may appear on underwear.

In both sexes, rectal gonorrhea may cause rectal pain during a bowel movement, and/or cause a cloudy discharge. Oral gonorrhea may cause a sore throat. Symptoms are usually not pronounced in such cases.

Often there are no marked symptoms either in males or in females. Thus, an infected person can become an unknowing transmitter.

See CHLAMYDIAL INFECTIONS-SYMPTOMS, page 59; also see NONSPECIFIC URETHRITIS-SYMPTOMS, page 68.

Diagnosis

Only a bacterial culture of the discharge yields a certain diagnosis. With males, a physician can usually make a correct diagnosis on the basis of symptoms and a microscopic examination of the pus-like discharge. With females, a culture is always required.

Self-diagnosis delays effective diagnosis and is not advisable.

Professional diagnosis can be obtained from a physician or, in some locations, from a clinic or health department. The cost of a culture is approximately $10 to $15; the cost of other services varies.

A confirmatory diagnosis takes about 48 hours.

Treatment

In general, a single injection of 250 mg. of an antibiotic called Rocephin (a ceftriaxone) is adequate to cure non-complicated gonorrhea in both the male and female. The drug must be prescribed by a physician.

Antibiotic resistant gonococcal bacteria appear in about five percent of cases and require more extensive treatment.

Successful treatment of gonorrhea does not prevent re-infection.

Partner

When a person is diagnosed as having gonorrhea, any partner within the last 30 days must be informed of the diagnosis and promptly treated just the same as the infected person.

As long as bacteria are in the genital tract, gonorrhea can be transmitted to a sexual partner and abstinence is indicated. Several days after successful treatment gonorrhea cannot be transmitted.

At the end of treatment, the infected person is presumed cured; but treatment failures are possible; so, until a test-of-cure shows that a cure has been effected, any sexual partner should be protected by use of a condom. See FOLLOW UP, below.

Once the infected person is cured, partner protection is not needed.

Follow-up

In order to detect treatment failures and re-infections, a re-examination and laboratory culture after one or two months is advisable.

A person who is diagnosed as having gonorrhea should also be tested for chlamydial infection, syphilis, AIDS, and hepatitis B.

Risks

It is not true that "The clap is no worse than a bad cold."

In males, untreated gonorrhea can spread to the prostate gland (prostatitis) and the epididymis (epididymitis), and the urethra can become scarred and narrowed, making urination difficult.

In females, untreated gonorrhea can become pelvic inflammatory disease (PID) by spreading to the uterine lining (endometritis) and the Fallopian tubes (salpingitis), and result in sterility, ectopic pregnancy, and continuing pelvic pain. It can infect the uterus and the surrounding abdominal cavity, and result in peritonitis.

Untreated gonococcal bacteria can spread to cause arthritis with pain and swelling in various joints. Multiplication of such bacteria in the blood stream can spread finally to cause death.

Treated gonorrhea is not fatal.

See CHLAMYDIAL INFECTIONS-RISKS, page 61; also see NONSPECIFIC URETHRITIS-RISKS, page 69.

Incapacitation

Both males and females can become physically incapacitated by gonorrhea, by complications discussed in RISKS, above.

Transmission

Gonorrhea has a short incubation period of from two to ten days. It is transmitted usually by sexual intercourse and by anal and oral sex.

Although transmission of gonorrhea by warm secretions from the genital area to unwashed hands, toilet seats, and the like are known to have occurred, such transmissions are rare and very unlikely to occur.

Avoidance

The use of a condom in sexual engagement reduces the risk of contracting or transmitting gonorrhea, for both males and females, but does not eliminate such risk.

There is no female copulatory device effective in reducing the risk of transmission. However, certain vaginal contraceptive foams and jellies decrease such risk; and some oral contraceptives decrease the incidence of cervical infection by gonorrhea in females.

There is no salve or pill to prevent infection of a male, except an antibiotic pill which is active against gonorrhea.

Incidence

Gonorrhea is the most frequently reported (but not the most frequently occurring) communicable disease in the United States, and has been so for many years.

In 1989, over 730,000 new cases were reported to the Centers for Disease Control. However, not all cases are reported; one CDC estimate places the true number of new cases at over 1.5 million a year.

The total number of cases of antibiotic resistant gonorrhea reported in 1989 was almost 56,000. This was a 50% increase in such cases from 1988; and fourteen times the number of such cases in 1984, five years earlier.

NONSPECIFIC URETHRITIS

Urethritis that is neither *gonorrhea* nor *chlamydial infection.* Nonspecific urethritis originally referred to urethritis that was nongonococcal. However, it is now known that about half of what used to be called nongonococcal urethritis was caused by Chlamydia trachomatis, and was in fact a chlamydial infection.

Who's Affected

Males are primarily infected, although female infection is not unknown.

Cause

In 70 to 80% of the cases of nonspecific urethritis, the infecting organism is simply never known. In the rest of the cases, the cause is the Ureaplasma urealyticum bacterium, the Trichomonas vaginalis protozoa (one of the causes of vaginitis), or the herpes simplex virus (the cause of genital herpes).

Symptoms

The incubation period of nonspecific urethritis is about two or three weeks.

After this period, males may have no symptoms but still be infected. More likely, males will have an urethral discharge, which may be cloudy or which may contain pus.

Females also may have no symptoms, but many will produce a vaginal discharge.

Both sexes may suffer chronic discomfort, burning upon urination, increased frequency of urination, and general discomfort in the pelvic area.

See CHLAMYDIAL INFECTIONS-SYMPTOMS, page 59; also see GONORRHEA-SYMPTOMS, page 63.

Diagnosis

Nonspecific urethritis is diagnosed by examination of the urine and by laboratory tests. Such tests, however, may not reveal the specific cause of the inflammation, though laboratory cultures of the urine may be helpful after a few days.

Sometimes one partner in sexual activity, who has no symptoms, can nevertheless be diagnosed as having nonspecific urethritis if the other partner has been diagnosed as having the disease.

Treatment

Treatment of nonspecific urethritis is difficult because in 70 to 80% of the cases the cause is unknown. The treatment failure rate is estimated to be 15%.

Often oral tetracycline is prescribed, and this treatment should be for at least ten days. This generic drug is inexpensive; however, generic medications can sometimes be less effective than their proprietary versions.

Successful treatment of nonspecific urethritis does not prevent re-infection.

Partner

When a person is diagnosed as having nonspecific urethritis, any recent partner must be informed of the diagnosis and promptly treated just the same as the infected person.

Since treatment of the infected person lasts at least ten days, and since it is not known at what point during these days the person becomes incapable of transmitting the disease, any sexual partner during the treatment period should be protected by abstinence, or at least by use of a condom.

At the end of treatment, the infected person is presumed cured; but treatment failures are possible; so, until a test-of-cure shows that a cure has been effected, any sexual partner should be protected by use of a condom. See FOLLOW UP, below.

Once the infected person is cured, partner protection is not needed.

Follow-up

Recurrences of nonspecific urethritis (sometimes followed by cystitis) are common, so that follow-up examinations of urine and discharges for three months are necessary.

A person who is diagnosed as having nonspecific urethritis should also be tested for chlamydial infection, gonorrhea, syphilis, AIDS, and hepatitis B.

Risks

Following nonspecific urethritis, both males and females can suffer complications.

In males, scarring, narrowing, and stricture of the urethra may occur. Cystitis, epididymitis, and prostatitis are common. About 5% of the cases of nonspecific urethritis will develop Reiter's syndrome, which is nonspecific urethritis plus arthritis and conjunctivitis.

In females, salpingitis, cervicitis or cystitis are common.

See CHLAMYDIAL INFECTIONS-RISKS, page 61; also see GONORRHEA-RISKS, page 65.

Incapacitation

Nonspecific urethritis is not physically incapacitating if treated promptly.

Transmission

Nonspecific urethritis is transmitted by sexual intercourse and by contact with ordinary skin, oral, and fecal bacteria.

It is possible but highly unlikely that it would be transmitted by contact with toilet seats.

Avoidance

Washing with soap and water before and after sexual intercourse and the use of a condom reduces the risk of contracting or transmitting nonspecific urethritis but does not eliminate such risk.

There are no salves, douches or pills that are effective in preventing the transmission of this disease for either males or females.

Incidence

The Centers for Disease Control estimate that, in 1989 in the U.S., there were 1.2 million new cases of nonspecific (nongonococcal, nonchlamydial) urethritis.

SYPHILIS

Commonly called *syph*; less commonly called the
pox, the great pox, lues, bad blood, haircut, old joe.

Who's Affected

Males and females alike can be infected without regard
to age.

Syphilis may be congenital (existing at birth); the
disease can be transmitted by an infected mother to an
unborn child.

Cause

Syphilis is an infection caused by Treponema pallidum,
a spirochete (spiral-shaped) bacterium.

Symptoms

Syphilis develops in three stages and can last
throughout a lifetime if untreated.

The symptom of the first stage of syphilis is a small,
painless sore called a chancre (pronounced "shanker"), that
is red, solid, and protruding above the skin. The chancre
usually appears three to four weeks after contact. If the
sore is on the penis, it is usually visible; if the sore is internal (the vagina in females, and the urethra, rectum and
mouth for both sexes) it is more difficult to detect. The
chancre heals four to eight weeks after appearance, and
leaves a thin scar. During the first stage, the infecting
bacteria are circulating throughout the body in the blood
stream.

Second stage symptoms begin about six to twelve
weeks after infection, and include a general feeling of illness,
fever, headache, and loss of appetite. Glands in the neck,
armpit, and groin may swell. Many persons also develop a
variety of skin conditions that include a rash of small,
scaling red bumps that do not itch, spots on the palms and
soles, gray plaques in the mucous membranes of the mouth,

vulva, or penis, and a rash around the rectum. These conditions are caused by the spread of the bacteria to body tissue. Sometimes, but rarely, syphilis infects the liver, eye, and meninges. All of these skin conditions are highly infectious. The second stage often lasts for about a year. See CHANCROID-SYMPTOMS, page 56; also see GENITAL HERPES-SYMPTOMS, page 86.

The third stage (neurosyphilis) begins two years after the disappearance of second stage symptoms, and lasts from two years to a lifetime. Its symptoms can be: paralysis, senility or dementia, loss of equilibrium, loss of feeling in the legs, and, sometimes, blindness. Syphilis can weaken the walls of the aorta and cause an aneurysm, and sometimes it even disturbs the functioning of the aortic valve of the heart.

Central nervous system disease may occur early or late in the course of syphilis.

Diagnosis

Primary syphilis is readily diagnosed by microscopic examination of the spirochetes in the chancre serum. In later stages, diagnosis is by blood tests.

Microscopic examinations are made in pathological laboratories such as in clinics, medical schools, and hospitals. Blood is tested in hospital and health department laboratories throughout the country; such tests take about two days and cost about $10. Office visits with private physicians cost from about $15 to $30; such visits to a health department clinic cost less.

All pregnant females should be screened for syphilis.

Treatment

In stages one and two, syphilis can be cured with prescription antibiotic injections, usually penicillin; if the patient is allergic to penicillin, another antibiotic may be effective.

Generally a single injection of penicillin, promptly administered, will effect a cure; it is relatively inexpensive. In lieu of penicillin, erythromycin or tetracycline may be used but neither is as effective as penicillin.

After successful treatment, a person is no longer a transmitter of syphilis.

However, the treatment of syphilis is not danger-free; the sudden killing of large numbers of spirochetes causes a severe reaction in more than one-half the persons treated. This is accompanied by fever, chills, headache, and muscular pain.

In stage three, if the infection has reached the brain and blood vessels, syphilis may not be curable.

Successful treatment of syphilis does not prevent re-infection.

Partner

When a person is diagnosed as having syphilis, any partner within the last 90 days must be informed of the diagnosis and promptly treated just the same as the infected person.

After treatment, the infected person is presumed cured; but treatment failures are possible; so, until a test-of-cure shows that a cure has been effected, any sexual partner should be protected by use of a condom. See FOLLOW UP, below.

Once the infected person is cured, partner protection is not needed.

Follow-up

Since treatment failures can occur, persons should be re-examined at three and six month intervals after initial treatment.

A person who is diagnosed as having syphilis should also be tested for AIDS and hepatitis B.

Risks

Untreated syphilis leads to death. Treating syphilis can avoid death, but depending upon the extent of the infection and the delay of treatment, damage to infected tissue may result. Organ damage, once incurred, sometimes cannot be reversed.

It is very important to diagnose and treat syphilis promptly as the sooner it is brought under control the more the likelihood of a complete cure.

A treated person will either be cured, or not cured. If not cured, syphilis becomes latent; the consequences are described under SYMPTOMS, above.

Incapacitation

There is minimal physical incapacitation from syphilis in males and females alike, if treatment is prompt. In the tertiary or third stage, physical incapacitation can be total, and social stigma severe as well.

Transmission

Syphilis if untreated goes through three prolonged stages: the first or primary stage produces a local sore; the second stage includes a diffuse rash; and the third stage, or neurosyphilis, involves the brain. See SYMPTOMS, above.

Syphilis is infectious in its primary and secondary stages, but not in its third stage.

Syphilis is transmitted directly by sexual activity, including sexual intercourse and oral and anal sex.

In males, the bacteria easily penetrate the walls of the urethra; in females, the bacteria easily penetrate the walls of the vagina. In all persons, the linings of the mouth and of the rectum, and the skin itself, are susceptible to initial penetration.

The incubation period is normally from two to three weeks, and can be as long as eight weeks; but within hours after infection the organism spreads to all parts of the body.

Avoidance

The use of a condom during intercourse and in anal sex reduces the risk of contracting syphilis, for both males and females, but does not eliminate such risk.

To insure avoidance of transmission by mouth and anus, refraining from oral and anal sex is advisable.

Incidence

Syphilis is the third most frequently reported (but not the third most frequently occurring) communicable disease in the United States; it is surpassed in reporting only by gonorrhea and chicken pox.

In 1989, over 110,000 new cases of syphilis in all stages were reported to the Centers for Disease Control. When the undiagnosed and/or untreated cases are considered, it is believed that the 1989 total is well over the reported cases. The infectious primary and secondary stages of syphilis accounted for about 40% of all cases.

About 44% more males than females contract syphilis. The incidence of cases of primary and secondary syphilis per 100,000 of population is greatest in large cities, and greater in southern states than in northern states.

VAGINITIS

A term used to refer to various infections of the vagina that do not involve the urinary tract. Commonly called *trick*, *TV* (*trichomoniasis*), and *fungus, vaginal thrush* (*yeast infection*).

Who's Affected

Females are affected by such vaginal infections, especially sexually active ones. Males can transmit such infections. See PARTNER, below.

Cause

The causes of vaginitis can be many, including allergies, hormone deficiencies, tampons, spermicidal creams, chemicals in douches, soaps, bath oils and salts, and common skin bacteria.

The three principal causes of vaginitis are: Trichomonas vaginalis protozoa; Candida albicans fungi (yeast infection; also called moniliasis); or Gardnerella vaginalis bacteria (nonspecific vaginitis). However, ordinary skin and fecal bacteria may be introduced into the vagina to cause vaginitis, also.

Symptoms

Generally, the symptoms of all kinds of vaginitis are itching, burning, pain during intercourse, and a vaginal odor and discharge.

Trichomonas infection involves a profuse, bad smelling yellow discharge, and may involve cervical sores.

Yeast infection involves a discharge that resembles cottage cheese with no strong odor; the most noticeable symptom is itching of the vulva.

Gardnerella infection involves a white or grayish and foul smelling discharge that may coat the vaginal walls; there may also be burning or itching.

Diagnosis

Vaginitis is diagnosed by analysis of the symptoms, sometimes confirmed by pelvic examination and a laboratory culture of the discharge.

Vaginitis can often be diagnosed promptly in the physician's office by microscopic examination of a wet smear of the vaginal secretions. Such an examination can reveal the presence of Trichomonas vaginalis, yeast, and nonspecific vaginitis.

Laboratory diagnoses for Trichomonas and yeast take approximately five days. Professional diagnosis costs between $20 and $35.

Diagnosis should be by a professional, such as a urologist, for example, trained in female genital tract diseases.

Treatment

Treatment for Trichomonas infection is usually a single, large oral dose of Flagyl; less often, an intravenous dose. All other forms of treatment are less efficient.

Yeast infection treatments have involved an antifungal prescription drug in a one to seven day course of therapy, depending on the severity of the infection. However, late in 1990 and early in 1991, the U.S. Food and Drug Administration (FDA) approved for over-the-counter sale Gyne-Lotrimin (clotrimazole) and Monistat 7 (miconazole nitrate) for the treatment of yeast infection.

Sulfa drugs or antibiotics usually cure Gardnerella infection.

The medication for treatments costs between $15 and $25.

Partner

When a female is tested positive for vaginitis, a physician should decide whether or not the nature of the infection requires a male partner to be treated. Vaginal infections rarely cause symptoms in a male, but the male partner can become infected and re-infect the female; he will require treatment if infected to prevent such re-infection.

Follow-up

Although proper treatment usually clears up a vaginal infection in about a week, repeated attacks can occur requiring re-evaluation and retreatment.

Risks

Treated vaginal infections are not considered to be dangerous although they often cause itching, a burning sensation during urination, and pain.

Untreated vaginitis can cause upper genital tract disease, which is called pelvic inflammatory disease (PID). This is serious; vaginal infections should be treated promptly.

Sometimes untreated vaginitis results in infections of the Bartholin's or Skene's glands, which, too, are painful and serious.

Incapacitation

Vaginitis usually is not physically incapacitating, but the complications are, as mentioned in RISKS, above.

Vaginitis's odor may be suppressed by a perfume douche and/or by washing; however, medical diagnosis and treatment for a cure is advisable.

Transmission

Vaginal infections are often transmitted by sexual intercourse and direct contact; but also are fostered by poor hygiene, deficient diet, or simple irritation of the vagina.

Frequently, a female may become self-infected; that is, she may have a yeast present in the gastro-intestinal tract, and develop a vaginal infection from yeast from the anal area that enters her vagina. Also, the use of antibiotics may decrease numerous usual bacteria within the vagina leaving yeast to overgrow, thus to cause a yeast infection.

Avoidance

Washing with soap and water before and after sexual intercourse and the use of a condom reduces the risk of contracting or transmitting sexually transmitted vaginitis, but does not eliminate such risk. However, see CAUSE, above.

The chance of contracting non-sexually transmitted vaginitis can be minimized by careful hygiene (particularly in the genital area), by a balanced diet, and by the avoidance of vaginal irritants.

The chance of contracting yeast infection can be minimized by the use of cotton underpants which breathe, rather than nylon ones which do not breathe and which promote dampness conducive to fungal growths.

The use of feminine hygiene sprays or powders, or douches, more than once weekly can kill the usual bacteria that suppress the yeast infection.

There are medications that can be taken before or after intercourse to decrease the chance of contracting vaginitis. The use of various antibiotics or specific antifungal or antitrichomonal medication will prevent the transmission of vaginitis for both males and females.

Incidence

As many as one-third of all females will be infected by some type of vaginitis during their lifetimes.

For 1988, the Centers for Disease Control report about 750,000 office visits to private physicians for trichomonal vaginitis, and about 9,500,000 such visits for vaginitis other than trichomonal. The twenty-year trend for trichomoniasis is gradually decreasing, and for non-trichomonal is sharply increasing.

Vaginitis probably accounts for more physician visits by females of reproductive age than any other sexually transmitted disorder.

AIDS

Acquired Immune Deficiency Syndrome,
commonly called *AIDS*.

AIDS is a new disease of the 1980's. While much is known about it, much is unknown. Because there is now no known cure or vaccine, and because fully developed cases are always fatal, extreme caution should be exercised to avoid infection.

Who's Affected

Males and females can be infected, primarily male homosexuals, especially promiscuous ones. There is evidence that AIDS is also affecting heterosexuals. IV (intravenous) drug abusers are especially at risk. At one time, hemophiliacs were at risk, though this risk has abated.

A fetus, infected by its mother, becomes a baby born with the disease.

Cause

AIDS is a late manifestation of an infection by a virus called human immunodeficiency virus. The virus is commonly referred to as HIV, the AIDS virus. When the disease was first defined as such, the virus was called human T cell lymphotropic virus III (HTLV III).

Symptoms

Most people infected with HIV remain asymptomatic (without symptoms) for months or even years; and many infected persons are unaware that they are infected. Others may have relatively mild complaints, such as weight loss, fever, sweating or diarrhea.

The time between infection with HIV and the development of AIDS ranges from a few months to more than 10 years. It is not known whether or not all persons infected with HIV will eventually develop full-blown AIDS.

AIDS ultimately involves a breakdown of the body's immune system, and this in turn allows invasion of the body by microbes that normally would be repelled. It is these secondary, opportunistic diseases that lead to death. Most common of such diseases are an especially virulent form of pneumonia, Kaposi's sarcoma (a rare skin cancer), dementia, meningitis, herpes simplex infection, destructive retinal infections inside the eye, and other serious, uncommon infections by bacteria, viruses, and fungi. From onset until death, full-blown AIDS usually lasts six months.

Sometimes in a person infected with HIV the combined symptoms of weight loss, fever, and enlarged lymph glands are termed AIDS-related complex, or ARC. Many if not all cases of ARC develop into full-blown AIDS. The ARC stage may last one to two years.

Diagnosis

A physician makes the diagnosis for HIV. The initial blood test is a screening test for antibodies costing about $20. If the initial test is positive, there follows a confirmatory test costing about $60. It takes approximately one week to do both tests.

Antibody tests cannot detect an HIV infection that occurred in the several weeks before the tests.

Confirmation of full-blown AIDS consists of confirmed HIV infection together with positive diagnosis of one or more of the secondary, opportunistic diseases.

HIV pre-test and post-test counseling is highly desirable.

Treatment

The only prescription drug approved by the U.S. Food and Drug Administration (FDA) for the treatment of AIDS is the antiviral drug AZT (zidovudine), sold under the trade name Retrovir. AZT is believed to slow the onset of full-blown AIDS and to alleviate some of the symptoms of the disease such as mental confusion and memory loss; but it is not a cure.

Currently, treatment with some experimental drugs, particularly DDI or dideoxyinosine (chemically related to AZT), has resulted in an indicated fall in virus levels, but such a fall is also not a cure.

The secondary diseases respond to drug and/or radiation treatment to a degree, but as yet there is no known treatment to rid the body of the AIDS virus and to restore its immune system. Treatment for secondary diseases is generally expensive, and debilitating.

It is not known how long AZT treatment can be helpful. However, late in 1989 it was learned that the prophylactic use of AZT can be beneficial with a 50% reduction in the dose. This, coupled with a 50% decrease in the price, has made AZT more practical for people who have been exposed to HIV. Therefore, it is possible that this treatment could be helpful for years. Since the treatment is not a cure, it is used only as a palliative to curb and slow the disease.

Since AZT has the ability to decrease virus counts and is believed to slow the attack of HIV on the immune system, although it is not therapeutic in the sense of effecting a cure, it is valuable to prolong life.

From AZT treatment many persons suffer adverse side effects, such as severe anemia, and experience interference with other drugs taken to treat the opportunistic diseases.

Partner

Past sexual and needle sharing partners of a person newly tested positive for HIV should be contacted for counseling and testing.

A spouse or future partner should not be exposed unknowingly to the risk of contracting HIV from a known HIV positive partner. If either sexual partner is HIV positive, disclosure of that fact to the other is of critical importance.

To reduce risk if one partner is HIV positive, condoms should be used in any episodes of sexual intercourse; and other precautions, such as those under AVOIDANCE, below, should certainly be taken. To eliminate risk, total abstinence is required.

The female who is HIV sero-positive should be warned of the fact that she will carry and can transmit the virus in all of her secretions including cervical and vaginal ones as well as in her blood stream.

She should be informed that if she elects to become pregnant, there is approximately a 40% chance that the fetus will become infected in utero.

Follow-up

Persons who test positive for HIV but who have not developed full-blown AIDS should seek regular post-test counseling and medical evaluations, perhaps at 1, 2, 3, 6, 9, and 12 month intervals.

The follow-up treatment of full-blown AIDS is progressive.

A person who is diagnosed as having AIDS should also be tested for chlamydial infection, gonorrhea, syphilis, and hepatitis B.

Risks

To date, all known fully developed cases of AIDS have led to death.

Incapacitation

A person who is HIV positive is not at first physically incapacitated and appears to be normal. However, the person who develops full-blown AIDS is a very sick and weak individual, who becomes wholly incapacitated.

Transmission

Sexually, HIV is transmitted by intercourse and by oral and anal sex. All persons with a positive blood test for antibodies to the virus are presumed to be capable of transmitting it.

It may be transmitted to a female by artificial insemination if the semen used is infected.

Non-sexually, HIV is transmitted by infected blood; hence, intravenous injections by a shared needle may transmit the virus. Also, the transfusion of infected blood will transmit the disease.

Experts disagree about whether HIV can be transmitted by saliva, tears, and other body fluids. Semen and blood are the principal proven transmitters; however, cases of transmission by female secretions are known. See PARTNER, above.

Avoidance

There is only one way to avoid sexually transmitted AIDS with absolute certainty, and that is to avoid the initial infection with HIV. There are only two ways of avoiding the initial infection with absolute certainty and they are:

(1) sexual abstinence; or

(2) choosing a sex partner who, for sure, is not infected with HIV.

The American Medical Association's *Encyclopedia of Medicine* (New York: Random House, 1989) contains the following comprehensive recommendations for preventing the spread of AIDS:

- Do not have sexual intercourse with persons known or suspected of having AIDS, with many people, or with people who have had many partners.

- Do not use intravenous (IV) drugs. If you use IV drugs, do not share needles or syringes.

- Do not have sex with people who use IV drugs.

- People with AIDS or who have had positive HIV antibody test results may pass the disease on to others and should not donate blood, plasma, body organs, other tissues or sperm. They should not exchange body fluids during sexual activity.

- There is a risk of infecting (or being infected by) others through sexual intercourse, sharing needles, and, possibly, exposure of others to saliva through oral-genital contact or "wet" kissing. The effectiveness of condoms in preventing infection with HIV is not proved, but their consistent use may reduce transmission, since exchange of body fluids is known to increase risk.

- Toothbrushes, razors, or other implements that could become contaminated with blood should not be shared.

However, it has been determined that a person cannot contract HIV from an infected person in a normal social relationship. HIV is not spread by touching, hugging, breathing or by the sharing of household items such as cutlery or tableware.

Incidence

AIDS was officially identified as a distinct disease in 1981.

Compared to some other sexually transmitted diseases, the number of known cases of AIDS in the United States is still small; however, the rate of increase in the number of cases is great.

Every year from 1 to 5 percent of those infected with HIV develop active AIDS. The Centers for Disease Control estimate that through 1989, there were one million HIV infected persons in the United States.

New data indicate that HIV is rapidly spreading among some groups of teenagers, equally between males and females, from heterosexual intercourse.

The disease has reached epidemic proportions in parts of Africa and Haiti.

By July of 1989, 100,000 AIDS cases had been reported in the United States to the Centers for Disease Control. The first 50,000 cases were reported in the six years from 1982 through 1987; the second 50,000 cases were reported in approximately one and one-half years, from December, 1987, through July, 1989. From July, 1989, through July, 1990, approximately 39,000 cases were reported.

GENITAL HERPES

Often simply called *herpes*.

Who's Affected

Males and females alike can be infected, but females are especially burdened by herpes infection: their initial disease is often more severe than males'; they suffer complications of pregnancy; and herpes may enhance the development of cervical cancer.

If a mother has active herpes when the baby is born, the baby can be infected during delivery.

Cause

Genital herpes is an infection caused by the herpes simplex Type 2 virus, which is much like the virus that causes cold sores and eye infections, namely, herpes simplex Type 1.

Symptoms

In males, about six days after contact with an infected person, there may be pain, tenderness, or an itchy sensation in or near the penis, and these symptoms may be accompanied by fever, headache, or a generally ill feeling. Soon thereafter single and multiple blisters appear along the penis, or sometimes on the thighs or buttocks. The blisters burst to form painful ulcers, which last from one to three weeks. See CHANCROID-SYMPTOMS, page 56; also see SYPHILIS-SYMPTOMS, page 71.

In females, after the same six day incubation period, the pain, tenderness or itchy sensation begins in the vulva or vagina accompanied by fever, headache, or a generally ill feeling. The blisters which follow may form internally on the vagina or cervix, as well as the vulva; if internal, the blisters cannot be seen. They may also form externally on the thighs or buttocks. The ulcers last, as in males, from one to three weeks.

The virus may remain in the body after the ulcers heal, and about half the persons who contract genital herpes will have a recurrence in later months or years; the recurrences are usually less severe and in time the symptoms do not appear again. The virus may remain in some body tissues throughout life.

Diagnosis

Genital herpes is diagnosed by microscopic exami-nation of a scraping from a blister or an ulcer and by laboratory culture of the removed cells. A culture costs about $25, and is obtained from a health care provider dealing with the genital tract.

From four to seven days are usually necessary to reach a diagnosis. However, the culture should be continued in the laboratory for at least three weeks to detect small amounts of virus.

Self diagnosis is inadvisable because blisters may be caused by other conditions.

Treatment

There is no known cure for genital herpes, but the more promptly treatment is given, the more likely the treatment will reduce the severity of the attack. Analgesics such as aspirin may relieve the pain. Antiviral drugs such as acyclovir, which costs about $62 for 100 capsules, afford excellent control and are now known to decrease the number of recurrences.

Warm baths may reduce inflammation.

Females who have the disease should have Pap smears for cervical cancer every six months for two years after the last attack; and then yearly.

Partner

When a person is diagnosed as having genital herpes, any preceding sex partner should be informed of the diagnosis so that if the partner develops symptoms, the probable cause will be known when that person seeks diagnosis.

Any current or continuing partner should be protected by abstinence while lesions are present; by abstinence when the blisters are crusted over, or at least by the use of a condom for such time; and by use of a condom even after symptoms disappear.

Any new partner should be informed of the herpes diagnosis, and protected by use of a condom.

Follow-up

Daily treatment with oral acyclovir for as long as three years may reduce the frequency of recurrent herpes, but such treatment does not eradicate the infection. After three years of such treatment, recurrent episodes of herpes are not benefited by acyclovir.

A person who is diagnosed as having genital herpes should also be tested for chlamydial infection, gonorrhea, syphilis, AIDS, and hepatitis B.

Risks

The herpes virus can spread through the blood stream to infect other organs especially in persons who have lowered resistance, such as those with cancer, and kidney, lung, and blood disorders. In females, herpes infection leads to increased risk of cervical cancer. In pregnant females, there is serious risk of transmitting the virus to the newborn upon delivery; a Cesarean section is preventive. Systemic infection of a newborn can lead to blindness, mental retardation, and even death.

Occasionally, herpes encephalitis, which is life-threatening, develops from first episode infection, among both males and females. This requires hospitalization and intravenous drug therapy.

Incapacitation

Although inconvenienced and uncomfortable, an infected person is rarely physically incapacitated by herpes unless there is brain involvement.

Transmission

Genital herpes can be transmitted by direct contact; normally, however, it is transmitted by sexual contact, such as sexual intercourse, oral sex, and anal sex.

Rarely transmission can be by other than such sexual activities. The herpes virus is very sensitive to drying and temperature; but it is theoretically possible that secretions still warm on a toilet seat, coming in contact with broken skin, could infect. Also, it is known that herpes virus on the skin of one person, brought into contact with the broken skin of another, can be transmitted.

A person is infectious from approximately two days before the herpes blister appears and until the ulcer that follows the blister is entirely crusted over. See SYMPTOMS, above.

Avoidance

The use of a condom in sexual intercourse and anal sex reduces the risk of contracting or transmitting herpes, for both males and females, but does not eliminate such risk.

There are no salves, douches, or pills effective in the prevention of herpes.

Incidence

Genital herpes is almost epidemic in the United States. Physician visits for genital herpes infection increased almost ninefold from 1970 through 1988.

The Centers for Disease Control estimate that there are between 200,000 and 500,000 new cases of genital herpes in the U.S. annually, and that the overall prevalence is close to 30 million in a population of over 240 million, or about one in eight.

GENITAL WARTS

Also called *venereal warts*, or *fig warts*. In males, such warts are more specifically called *penile warts*; in females, *vulval warts*.

Who's Affected

Males and females alike can develop warts; but male children and teenagers are especially susceptible.

A baby born to a female with genital warts can be infected with the wart virus during delivery.

Cause

A wart is caused by an invading virus which causes the skin cells to multiply rapidly. Genital warts on males and females alike are caused by certain types of the human papilloma virus (HPV).

Symptoms

A wart is a small, hard or horny, benign lump on the surface of the skin, which may be white or pink in color. There are no indications of the development of a wart before its appearance; and it may take 18 months for the wart to develop after the infection.

A wart-like growth on the penis, or invisibly in the urethra, may be a symptom of cancer of the penis, or of syphilis.

Vulval warts may appear along with an increased vaginal discharge; and they may also occur during pregnancy when the moist conditions that promote them are increased naturally.

Diagnosis

Generally, external warts on both sexes can be diagnosed by inspection; there is no ability to culture the virus.

External warts on females are frequently accompanied by warts in the genital area, including the vagina and the cervix. Therefore, after the appearance of a wart, the entire genital tract should be examined. Internal warts are located by visual inspection, by use of a colposcope. Their existence is confirmed by microscopic examination of surgically removed specimens (biopsy).

Treatment

Warts in general are treated by a physician by cryo-surgery (freezing), electrodesiccation (drying), or curettage (scraping), by laser, or by the application of podophyllin. Some warts are treated with interferon.

There is no permanent cure for warts. After the external wart is removed, the virus is still present in the tissue. The virus may manifest itself again as overt warts, or as a subclinical infection, or in a form so as to cause abnormal cells to appear in a Pap smear.

Some over-the-counter wart paints are much too strong to be used on genital warts; the use of some such preparations may result in pain and scarring.

Partner

When a person is diagnosed as having genital warts, any preceding sex partner should be informed of the diagnosis and promptly examined.

It is difficult for a person infected with warts to protect a sex partner. If the warts are on the shaft of the penis or in the vagina, a condom will offer some protection. If the warts infect other genital areas, the condom affords no protection.

Any new partner should be informed of the warts diagnosis, and protected if possible.

Warts in the urethra or vagina may not be seen by partners.

Follow-up

Because no therapy has been shown to eradicate genital warts, and because they have a tendency to recur, an apparent cure should be under constant watch for possible recurrence.

Although one partner may be known to have genital warts, both partners in a continuing relationship should be checked and rechecked because the infection can be transmitted back and forth.

Risks

A risk lies in mis-diagnosis of something such as a surface cancer that appears to be a wart but is not; and also by mistreatment.

A long-neglected vulval wart can become malignant, but this is rare. There is some indication that a wart infection of a female's cervix is linked to cervical cancer. Such an infection will cause an abnormal Pap smear.

As said in WHO'S AFFECTED, above, a fetus can become infected with warts by its mother; such an infection is serious because it can cause warts in the baby's windpipe. It is not possible to determine which infected mother will transmit the virus.

Incapacitation

Generally, warts are physically incapacitating only if they become large. However, warts in the front of the body which bleed or become secondarily infected can be psychologically damaging because of the abnormal appearance created.

Transmission

Warts are transmitted by direct contact through breaks in the skin or mucosal lining, which allow the virus to enter.

It is not known how much virus is shed by a wart and therefore it is not known whether touching the wart will transmit the infection to unbroken skin. The incubation period of warts is also unknown.

Avoidance

The chance of developing a wart can be minimized by avoiding contact with a wart or the skin from a wart. The use of a condom in sexual engagements reduces the risk of contracting or transmitting genital warts, but does not eliminate such risk. Warts frequently occur in the genital area not protected by a condom.

Incidence

The Centers for Disease Control estimate that in 1988, there were 1,200,000 visits to private physicians for treatment of genital warts.

HEPATITIS B

Formerly called *serum hepatitis*; sometimes called *viral hepatitis type B*; sometimes called *liver infection*.

Who's Affected

Males and females alike can be infected; however, hepatitis B is particularly common among homosexual males; among heterosexuals with multiple partners; and among drug abusers.

A pregnant female may pass the virus on to a newborn at delivery; such a newborn is at high risk for contracting chronic hepatitis B.

Cause

Hepatitis B is an infection of the liver by the hepatitis B virus (HBV).

Symptoms

Symptoms of hepatitis B include: jaundice, weakness, loss of appetite, nausea, dark urine, abdominal discomfort, fever, and light stool. Some persons infected with HBV develop no symptoms; such persons become carriers able to transmit the virus to others, perhaps without knowing it.

Diagnosis

Hepatitis B is diagnosed by a blood test ordered by a physician; the test takes about two days, and costs about $15 to $20.

Treatment

For a person diagnosed definitely and with mild symptoms, rest and a high calory diet are usually prescribed. Recently, interferon by mouth has been used to inhibit growth of the virus. If symptoms are severe, oral steroids may be needed.

Generally, treatment, monitored by a physician, can be given at home.

In a small percentage of persistent cases, hospitalization is necessary for a series of blood tests to determine the probable progress of the disease.

Partner

When a person is diagnosed as having hepatitis B, any partner within the last 14 days must be informed of the diagnosis and given a prophylactic injection of hepatitis B immune globulin (HBIG), followed by hepatitis B vaccine treatment.

Because of the highly infectious nature of hepatitis B, a person with the disease should protect a sexual partner by disclosure and abstinence, or at least by disclosure and use of a condom, until the person is no longer infectious.

Household members should be protected by exceptional cleanliness and by avoiding the common use of items such as razors, toothbrushes and the like, that might contain infected blood. See AVOIDANCE, below.

Technically, as long as a person carries hepatitis B antigens in the blood, that person in infectious; but when tests show hepatitis B antibodies in the blood, the vast majority of such persons are no longer infectious and are considered cured; and the above precautions are no longer necessary. Antibodies may appear as soon as six weeks after the onset of the disease.

Follow-up

Hepatitis B progresses to become chronic in about ten percent of all cases. Therefore, after an initial positive blood test, additional tests are indicated from time to time to determine whether or not the disease will progress to require chronic treatment.

A person who is diagnosed as having hepatitis B should also have blood tests for AIDS.

Risks

Hepatitis B is a potentially dangerous disease to liver function and to life.

In a large proportion of cases, the virus persists for years, and ten percent of persons, male and female, with hepatitis B develop chronic liver disease.

Chronic liver disease is serious; usually cirrhosis of the liver is involved with progressive liver failure. In some cases, exceptionally serious liver cancer develops with less than a five year chance of survival.

Incapacitation

Even in less serious cases of hepatitis B, the normal course of which is only three to six months, the infected person, although not wholly physically incapacitated, is somewhat debilitated with a lack of energy.

Regarding more serious cases, see RISKS, above.

Transmission

Hepatitis B is transmitted sexually more often than any other way by contact with the sperm of an infected male, or the menstrual blood of an infected female.

Non-sexually, it is transmitted by contact with blood (wet or dry), saliva, and/or the nasal mucus of an infected person.

It is highly unlikely that it will be transmitted by contact with unwashed hands, toilet seats, or the like.

Hepatitis B can be transmitted by a carrier; that is, a person who is asymptomatic but infectious. It can be transmitted as long as the virus is present in the carrier's blood, which can be for the entire life of the carrier.

Avoidance

Vaccination against hepatitis B is possible. The vaccine is hepatitis B vaccine which must be prescribed, and which must be taken in three visits spread over six months. Surgeons, nurses, anesthesiologists, and others likely to come into contact with infected persons should be vaccinated, as well as multiple sex partners, homosexual men, and prostitutes.

The use of a condom in sexual engagement reduces the risk of contracting or transmitting hepatitis B, for both males and females, but does not eliminate such risk.

The risk of contracting non-sexually transmitted hepatitis B can be reduced by avoiding contact with the body fluids of an infected person; by not sharing needles; by avoiding ear piercing, tattooing, and the like unless the equipment is known to be sterile; and in general by cleanliness and by the same precautions used to reduce the risk of contracting HIV. See AIDS-AVOIDANCE, page 84.

A person travelling to a high incidence area on vacation or business may gain some temporary immunity by an injection of HBIG.

There are no salves, douches or pills effective in preventing the transmission of hepatitis B.

Incidence

The Centers for Disease Control: estimate 300,000 new cases of hepatitis B in the United States each year. The CDC also estimate the national pool of infectious hepatitis B carriers to be between 750,000 and 1,000,000 persons.

PUBIC LICE

Formally, *pediculosis pubis*. Also called
crab lice and, commonly, *crabs, cooties*.

Who's Affected

Males and females alike can be infested.

Cause

A proliferation of pubic lice (Pediculus pubis) on an
infested person is fostered by unsanitary personal habits
such as the failure to wash thoroughly and regularly with
soap and water. Lice are small, wingless, usually flattened
insects parasitic on warm-blooded animals.

Symptoms

It takes several weeks for the lice to breed and many
persons have no symptoms of pubic lice before the small
parasites appear in numbers; however, others have itching
in the infested region, especially at night.

Pubic lice are blood-sucking lice that usually appear
in pubic and anal hair, but can appear in other body hair,
the eyebrows and eyelashes. They are visible upon close
inspection; the louse is about 1/8 of an inch long when
mature.

The pale, white eggs of pubic lice, called nits, can be
seen with a magnifying glass and are tightly attached to
hairs.

There are other related lice, such as the body or head
louse.

Diagnosis

Pubic lice can be found by inspection; self-diagnosis,
is, of course, often possible.

Treatment

Pubic lice and eggs cannot be removed by ordinary soap and washing.

Over-the-counter lotions and ointments are available to kill the lice and remove eggs. With several treatments the lice and eggs are usually eliminated.

Also available is Kwell, a prescription lotion; its active ingredient is lindane, and it is relatively inexpensive.

Infestations of the scalp, eyebrows, or eyelashes require special ointments, and particular care in application to protect the eyes.

Contaminated clothing and bed linen should be machine washed (hot cycle) and dried, or dry cleaned. Mattresses concealing nits or lice in their crevices should be burned.

Partner

When a person is diagnosed as having pubic lice, any past sex partner must be informed of the diagnosis and promptly treated just the same as the infested person.

To prevent transmission, an infested person should avoid sexual contact; there is no other protection that can be offered.

Once the infested person is successfully treated, protection is not needed.

Follow-up

If nits or lice are found at the hair-skin juncture seven days after the initial treatment, topical retreatment is necessary.

Risks

There are normally no serious consequences from having an infestation of pubic lice. However, scratching to alleviate the itching can cause open sores and scabs. Since pubic lice flourish under unsanitary conditions, such sores can become infected by normal skin bacteria to create small boils or abscesses.

Incapacitation

Infestation by pubic lice incapacitates neither sex, physically.

Transmission

Pubic lice are transmitted by direct contact of genital hair in sexual intercourse, or in anal sex. Lice also may be transmitted from the scalp, the eyelashes, and armpit hair.

Parents sometimes transmit lice to their children by unsanitary personal and household hygiene.

Pubic lice do not transmit infection.

Avoidance

There is no practical way of avoiding the transmission of pubic lice if a person engages in sexual intercourse or anal sex with an infested person.

Incidence

An authoritative source in private communication reports 127,000 visits to private physicians for pubic lice in 1989.

Since self-diagnosis and unreported treatment are relatively easy, it is thought that pubic lice are more widely spread than statistics indicate.

SCABIES
Sometimes called *the itch.*

Who's Affected

Males and females alike can be infested; scabies is most common among the young, refugees, and the institutionalized.

Cause

Scabies is a contagious skin disease caused by a mite, Sarcoptes scabiei, that flourishes in unsanitary conditions and that burrows into the skin where it lays its eggs. Mites are small to minute insects related to spiders and ticks.

Symptoms

Intense itching, usually at night, is the principal symptom of scabies.

Scabies occurs on the hands between the fingers, and on wrists, armpits, buttocks, and/or genitals. Scaly swellings on the skin, which are the mites' burrows, are often visible. Later, reddish lumps often appear on the skin.

Diagnosis

Scabies can sometimes be diagnosed by observing the skin tracks of moving mites; otherwise, by microscopic examination of recovered mites.

Self-diagnosis is not advisable because such diagnosis is hardly ever done correctly. The cost of professional diagnosis at a public health department clinic is nominal.

Treatment

Scabies is treated by careful washing; and by the application of a prescription medication to the entire body below the neck. Itching may continue for several weeks after successful treatment.

Normally, lindane lotion (which is sometimes sold under the brand name of Kwell, a prescription drug) is prescribed.

The mites die soon after removal from human skin; infested cloth can be cleansed by machine laundering, or by avoiding its use for at least four days.

Partner

When a person is diagnosed as having scabies, any sex partner and all household members must be informed of the diagnosis and promptly treated just the same as the infested person.

To prevent transmission, an infested person should avoid bodily and sexual contact; there is no other protection that can be offered.

Once the infested person is successfully treated, protection is not needed.

Follow-up

Retreatment after a week may be required; additional weekly treatments are warranted only if live mites can be identified.

Risks

There are normally no serious risks from scabies. However, scratching to alleviate itching can cause open sores and scabs; and since scabies sometimes results from overcrowded, unsanitary living conditions, the open sores that result from such scratching may become infected.

Incapacitation

Infestation by the scabies mite incapacitates neither sex, physically.

Transmission

Scabies is highly contagious and is transmitted by close personal contact, such as sharing a bed or clothing, or sexual contact with an infested person. Hatched mites can pass directly from an infested person to another person standing nearby, but are more likely to pass by physical contact.

Avoidance

The mites can be avoided by avoiding contact with an infested person, or with infested bedding or clothing.

Incidence

An authoritative source in private communication reports 759,000 visits to private physicians for scabies in 1989.

PREGNANCY

UNLAWFUL INTERCOURSE

Incest–Rape–Statutory Rape

Although in some quarters the recent trend in sexual matters has been toward anything goes (see ABOUT THE GLOSSARY, page 195), the violent crime of rape and the crimes of incest and statutory rape are still considered by society and the law as wrongful and abhorred.

Incest as a crime is sexual intercourse between persons closely related by blood or adoption and possibly by marriage; civil incest is marriage attempted between persons within the legally prohibited degrees of relationship by blood or marriage. See 22 INCEST.

Rape is sexual intercourse which is engaged in by forcible compulsion or against the will of another person or with a person who is incapable of consenting because of age or mental condition. See 23 SEXUAL HARASS-MENT; also see 24 RAPE.

Statutory rape is sexual intercourse between one person and another who is incapable of consenting because such person is below the minimum age set by the law for consent to sexual intercourse. See 25 STATUTORY RAPE.

There is a double taboo about incest: it's not to be done, and it's not to be talked about. The second part of the taboo has weakened in recent years; discussion about incest is emerging, and may be where discussion about rape was in the 1960s; such discussion then was almost non-existent. The emergence of incest as an important, discussable topic is likely to increase with the high rate of divorce and reconstituted families.

105

Rape is a crime of violence involving physical force, threats, or psychological intimidation. Often, the victim is raped by a person she knows—a neighbor, perhaps, a relative, or a date. Most rapists are repeaters.

The FBI estimates that one of every five females in the U.S. will be sexually assaulted at least once during her life. See 26 CASTRATION.

For victims who elect not to be treated by their personal physicians, there are available in almost all large cities Rape Relief Centers. These Centers recommend that victims should not bathe, douche, or change clothes in order not to wash away evidence (see 27 PROOF OF RAPE) such as semen; should not destroy evidence at the scene of the crime; should go to a hospital immediately; should take a change of clothes to the hospital because clothes worn when raped—especially underpants—may be needed for evidence; should expect tests at the hospital for semen and for existing pregnancy and venereal disease; and should call the police to meet at the hospital to give information that could be helpful in arresting and prosecuting the rapist.

Such Centers appropriately recommend a check for gonorrhea a week after the rape; and for syphilis 90 days after; however, antibiotics such as penicillin may be given immediately after the rape to prevent venereal infection.

A blood test for HIV, the virus that causes AIDS, is also advisable.

Many physicians advise an estrogen within 72 hours of the rape to bring on menstruation so that pregnancy does not result from the rape.

Rape Relief Centers encourage victims to report rapes and if the victim elects to testify for the prosecution, the state, not the victim, will hire the prosecuting attorney and the Center will accompany the victim through the court procedure.

Consent, or blame-the-victim, is the rapist's usual defense. When the rapist is an acquaintance or a date, the victim should avoid confusing the consent issue by feeling that she should have prevented the assault. If she in fact is not to blame, she should not let self criticism or doubt interfere with action.

On the other hand, if she in fact did consent, then there was no rape, and she should remember that there are severe legal penalties for all false accusations including a false accusation of rape. See 28 FALSE ACCUSATION.

Fornication-Adultery

The increased acceptance by some people of cohabitation with sex, and perhaps with "commitment" but without marriage, may or may not be an advance in social standards. Although the opprobrium that formerly attended fornication has largely vanished, this non-violent activity is still illicit in some jurisdictions.

Adultery is, of course, a far more serious offense by social, and in some states legal, standards.

> Fornication is voluntary sexual intercourse between two unmarried persons. See 29 FORNICATION.

> Adultery is voluntary sexual intercourse between a married person and someone not his or her legal spouse. See 30 ADULTERY.

If such intercourse is between a married and an unmarried person, the married person is considered an adulterer and the unmarried person may be considered a fornicator.

The remaining laws against fornication are rarely enforced. The legal penalties for adultery have become less severe, generally; for example, in most jurisdictions, adultery is now irrelevant to obtaining a divorce and to property division. The concept of no-fault divorce is more and more widely spread.

The penalties for fornication are now likely to be more personal than legal; the penalties for adultery can be both legal and personal. Broken family relationships, such as divorce, frequently follow adultery. Abortions, or single parenthoods, which can be wrenching, are often the aftermath of fornication. See UNWANTED PREGNANCIES, page 167.

22 INCEST

Medical

Traditional medical reasons for legal prohibitions against incest include the belief that inbreeding among members of a family can result in congenital defects. For example, when close blood relatives such as first cousins marry, the chance that their child will inherit birth defects is, traditionally, believed to be increased.

However, the validity of the traditional belief is not accepted now by all experts; it is said by some that modern genetic science does not support the theory. It should be noted that such a statement does not advocate incest, rather merely questions the traditional medical reasons for the legal prohibition. Nevertheless, if a child is conceived in incest, the Medical Editors believe that a termination of pregnancy should be considered.

"Incest cuts across socioeconomic and racial lines and is much more common than was previously thought.

"For an adolescent victim of incest (or, as is frequently the case, of repeated acts of incest) there is often, in addition to the abuse itself, a further distress: The perpetrator of the act is someone who in all other areas is a source of love and support. The most common pairings are father-daughter, uncle (or other adult male)-niece. More rarely, the act involves an older brother and a sister. Male victims, however, also exist and should not be forgotten, since they may be less willing to seek help.

"In the past, incest was surrounded by silence. The alternatives for the victims were to run away from home, to wait until they had homes of their own to move to, or, more rarely, to retaliate with violence. Today, there is a slowly growing willingness to discuss the problem and to try to organize care and help for the victims." (The Columbia University College of Physicians and Surgeons, *Complete Home Medical Guide*, [New York: Crown, 1985], 243)

Legal

Incest means sexual intercourse between persons within the prohibited degrees of family relationships. Criminal incest is a serious crime (a felony).

States vary in delineating which relationships fall within the prohibited degrees. Direct relationships between ancestors and descendants, of any degree, will fall within the prohibition: parent, grandparent, great grandparent, etc., and child, grandchild, greatgrandchild, etc. Collateral relationships between siblings (brother and sister) will always be included. Other collateral relationships may be included: uncle-niece, aunt-nephew, cousins of varying degrees. Criminal incest statutes will also apply to children by adoption and their adoptive families and may also apply to step-parent and step-child.

The prohibition of sexual intercourse between family members is also the basis for the prohibition of marriage (civil incest) on the basis of consanguinity (blood relationship) and affinity (relationship by marriage). States always forbid marriage between ancestor and descendant, by blood or adoption: parent-child, grandparent-grandchild, etc. States also always forbid marriage between siblings by blood; today some states allow marriage between brother and sister by adoption. In the case of collateral blood relatives (uncle-niece, aunt-nephew, or cousins) and of relations by marriage (in-laws, stepparent-stepchild), each state draws its own lines concerning which relationships will fall within the prohibition of marriage on the basis of family relationship.

Ethical

In Judaism incest is forbidden. Leviticus 18:6-10 details a long list of incestuous relationships which are forbidden. No specific reason for the prohibition is given. In general, incestuous practices were apparently considered to be idolatrous and a violation of the person's relationship to God and to fellow Israelites. The punishment was: "For whoever shall do any of these abominations, the persons that do them shall be cut off from their people." (Leviticus 18:20) The power of excommunication was also a penalty.

In Islam, incest is forbidden. The reason for the strong prohibition is that "God proscribes for you." To violate God's proscription is to do harm to yourself and those around you. (Arberry Translation, Book I, Ch. IV, lines 28ff)

In Buddhism, incest would be a violation of Precept Three: To abstain from sexual misconduct. There are twenty kinds of women that a male is forbidden to "go into," meaning to have sexual relations with. Ten of them are women who are family relations. To have sexual relations with them is a misuse of one's own body and that of the relative as well; furthermore, these persons are under the protection of the potential offender and are not to be exploited sexually but protected by him.

In Christianity, there is a specific prohibition against incest in I Corinthians 5:1. The Apostle Paul expresses horror that one in the Corinthian church was having sex with his own mother. Paul levies the penalty: "Let him who has done this be removed from among you."

In most branches of Christianity today, incest is considered the worst form of sexual abuse. There are extensive pastoral care programs for the restoration of the abused person to emotional well-being. Care is offered the offender who has abused the other family member. However, pastors and other religious counselors are under some obligation to report these sex offenders to family protection agencies in many if not all states. (See Ellen Bass and Laura Davis, *The Courage to Heal*, [New York: Harper and Row, 1988], and James Leehan, *Pastoral Care of Survivors of Family Abuse*, [Louisville: Westminster-John Knox, 1989].)

Psychological

Either or both partners in an incestuous relationship may feel intense guilt even if the incest is undetected; if detected, the whole family dynamics are likely to be adversely affected.

Father-daughter incest where the daughter was unwilling, may be especially damaging psychologically to the daughter's future relationships with men; she may suffer guilt, low self-esteem, and fear or anger.

Children in incestuous situations are often terrorized not to tell; such children may as adults experience anxiety and fear in sexual relations.

Among delinquent girls and prostitutes, a relatively high incidence of an incestuous background has been reported.

Disorders stemming from incest usually benefit from therapy.

23 SEXUAL HARASSMENT

Medical

There are no medical consequences that a female will suffer if subjected to sexual harassment, unless the harassment involves violence, or sexual encounter; the latter raises the possibility of disease and/or unwanted pregnancy if intercourse is involved.

Legal

Sexual harassment is a form of discrimination based upon sex which is forbidden by the Civil Rights Act of 1964 with respect to employment. The sexual harassment which is prohibited is found in two forms: (i) the conditioning of concrete employment benefits (hiring, job transfer, promotion, increase in salary or benefits) upon sexual favors; or (ii) the creation of a hostile or offensive work environment. The offensive work environment is one in which there are unwelcome sexual advances, requests for sexual favors, or other verbal or physical conduct of a sexual nature if the conduct has the purpose or effect of interfering with an individual's work performance. The hostile work environment may be created by sexual jokes, references, or innuendo, when these create an environment which is unwelcome. Local governments and educational institutions are developing laws and rules which forbid harassment of individuals on the basis of race, religion, gender or ethnic origin. If such laws and regulations are found to be consistent with the First Amendment protection for free speech, conduct which in the past may have been considered as merely "locker room talk" or "typical male jokes and remarks" will be found to violate the law and subject the speaker or actor to liability for harassment.

Psychological

Sexual harassments may vary from unwelcome but persistent whistles, leers, pinches, touches, frottages (rubs), fondlings, or more serious sexual advances.

Sexually harassed persons may suffer anger, and sometimes guilt ("What did I do to bring this on me?"). If the harassment is of a subordinate in the workplace, the victim may feel not only anger and frustration, but also insecurity.

24 RAPE

Medical

Medical rape tests that are intended to be acceptable as evidence in court are classified as forensic tests. The American Medical Association's *Encyclopedia of Medicine* (New York: Random House, 1989), on page 850, describes such tests as follows: "The physician examining a rape victim performs a physical examination, noting signs of bruising or injury, particularly to the genital area. The examination includes inspection of the vaginal canal with a speculum. A woman is usually present to support the victim.

"For laboratory analysis, the physician collects swabs from any suspected bite marks, from soiled areas of the body, and from the vagina, anus or throat; fingernail scrapings or clippings; and any torn-out strands of head or pubic hair. These may be matched with samples of blood or saliva taken from suspects.

"Clothing worn by the victim at the time of the assault is also retained for forensic examination."

Legal

Forcible rape is an act of sexual intercourse against the will and without the consent of the victim. It should be distinguished from "statutory rape" which is sexual intercourse with a person below the age of legal consent. See 25 STATUTORY RAPE. If a victim is drugged, unconscious or mentally incompetent, intercourse with her is deemed to be rape. Rape is a serious crime (felony) in all states, and in most, can be committed only by a male upon a female. In some states, "sexual intercourse" is defined by statute to include not only penetration of the penis into the female genital organ, but also penetration into the mouth and anus.

Traditionally, marriage of the aggressor to his victim will be a defense to a rape charge on the theory that by contracting a marriage, a woman gives her continuing and irrevocable consent to have sexual relations with her husband. This rule is criticized because it ignores the interest of married women to be free from unwanted physical invasions. Nevertheless, only a few states have abolished the marriage defense to rape.

Many states have created degrees of rape, with penalties varying in accordance with the severity of the crime. However, rape of any degree may be penalized with long prison terms, as it is perceived to be a crime almost as serious as murder.

In addition to criminal liability, a rapist may be held liable to his victim in a civil suit for damages. Liability, both criminal and civil, may also arise if the rapist has transmitted a venereal disease to his victim. See 19 DAMAGES.

Ethical

Jewish law prohibits rape particularly if the woman is betrothed to another man and resists by crying out for help when accosted by a rapist. Rape was considered as a form of adultery on the part of the man without the consent of the woman. It was punished as adultery: "So you shall purge the evil from the midst of you." (Deut. 22:24) The penalty was death. (Lev. 20:13) Seduction of a virgin was seen as the crime of having stolen her virginity. A payment of fifty shekels to her father was required for having stolen her virginity; then the rapist was required to marry her: "...she shall be his wife because he has violated her; he shall not put her away all his days." It is noteworthy that the woman does not seem to have had any choice in either the sex act or in the marriage.

In Islam, the *Code du Statut Personnel* (a French translation from the Arabic), the criminal code of crimes and offenses against family order and public morality, mentions virginity in connection with rape. Rape is punishable by a five to ten year imprisonment; but if the woman was a virgin, the penalty is a ten to 20 year imprisonment. In American Islam, criminal justice laws of the state would be applicable.

In Buddhism, rape is the ultimate in sexual misconduct, a violation of Precept Three: To abstain from sexual immorality. The pain of life comes from craving for passion, of which rape is the worst. Such pain to oneself and to the assaulted person would cease by overcoming such craving. In American Buddhism, the criminal statutes against the rapist would most certainly be affirmed by the Buddhist.

The New Testament does not deal with the specific issue of rape. However, in post-biblical writings throughout Christian history there have been canonical laws against the rapist. In present day practice, rape has been left to secular criminal law. The function of the Christian community is to provide counseling, therapy, and protection for the raped woman as a person in her own right and to raise public consciousness against men who ravage women with rape.

Prison chaplains seek through individual and group counseling to extend redemptive wisdom and Christian love to the rapists themselves.

As a group, the major religions have little to say about spousal rape. In Christianity, there is an implied injunction against spousal rape in I Peter 3:7, "Husbands, ...show consideration for your wives in your life together, paying honor to the woman as the weaker sex since they too are also heirs of the gracious gift of life—so that nothing may hinder your prayers."

Similarly, homosexual rape is not mentioned by the major religions.

Psychological

In heterosexual rape, sexual pleasure and satisfaction is not the motivation; the motivation is the expression of anger or hatred and the rapist's satisfaction is derived from exercising power over his victim—power which often includes physical violence. Most rapists are attempting to raise their low self-esteem and to feel powerful by demeaning a helpless victim by using sex as a weapon.

Immediate post-rape counseling for the victim is important; longer term counseling is also indicated if stress reactions emerge, such as aversion to sexual activity, fear of men, loss of orgasmic function, fear of going outside (if the rape occurred outside), fear of being alone, or nightmares.

Rapists may be sociopathic, mentally retarded, intoxicated with drugs or alcohol, neurotic, sadistic, or otherwise normal.

The rapist should seek or be offered counseling. The success of such counseling varies with individual cases and is affected by the sincerity of the rapist's desire to change. However, there is at present a movement in the U.S. away from therapy and towards incarceration, indicating discontent with the results of therapy.

The victim's resistance is crucial to successful prosecution of the rapist.

25 STATUTORY RAPE

Legal

Statutory rape is sexual intercourse with a person who is below the age of legal consent. Typically, only females can be victims of statutory rape. The fact that the victim consented to intercourse or was actually the seducer is not a defense to a charge of statutory rape because the victim is held as a matter of law to be incapable of giving legal consent. Likewise, a defendant's reasonable belief that his partner was of legal age is not a defense. If a person is legally married to his partner, however, he cannot be charged under statutory rape laws.

If the rape was committed with force, a defendant would likely be charged as well under forcible rape statutes, which commonly incur harsher penalties. See 24 RAPE. If a defendant is related by blood or marriage to his victim, he may also be charged with criminal incest. See 22 INCEST.

In typical statutory language, the victim must be under a specified age (commonly 16), and the defendant must be a minimum number of years older than his victim (commonly four years). Some states create degrees of statutory rape, with severer penalties attached to sexual intercourse with extremely young females.

Ethical

Rabbinic law used moral persuasion to make the man who raped a minor marry her, though no legal compulsion was employed. In Islam, statutory rape would be most likely considered the violation of a virgin, and severe punishment would be meted out in a Moslem community. In American Buddhist and Islamic communities statutory rape would be considered much as it is in the Judaeo-Christian communities, that is as sexual abuse if done by a relative, and as premarital sex if done by a minor to a minor as in teenage sex. Legal recourse would be taken against the adult offender and pastoral care would be extended to the young victim.

Psychological

A "normal" adult male who commits statutory rape might or might not experience guilt, depending on many factors, including the emotional relationship between the minor female and the rapist, her willingness, and/or enjoyment, etc.

The minor, if consenting, might feel no adverse psychological reactions from statutory rape; or, depending upon her character, she might feel guilt, shame, and anger.

The rapist, the minor, and her parents should all seek counseling.

26 CASTRATION

Medical

Medically, castration is the removal of the male testes or the female ovaries and is important in the treatment of certain hormonal imbalances, malignant tumors, and other disorders of both sexes.

However, castration is not recommended as a treatment of, or a punishment for, rape.

Legal

Castration has been suggested as an appropriate penalty for repeat sexual offenders. Whether castration is acceptable may depend on the reason for its use. If ordered simply for retribution purposes, there is precedent in our law to hold that it is a cruel and unusual punishment, akin to torture, which is prohibited by the Eighth Amendment to the United States Constitution and by similar provisions found in state constitutions.

Castration may be proposed, not for retribution purposes, but as a means to deter future sexual offenses. Rape is a crime of violence. Some believe that there is a causal relationship between violent behavior and the level of male hormones produced by the testes. Therefore, removal of the testes may be a biological cure for sexually deviant behavior. There are two problems with employing castration for this purpose: (i) there is insufficient scientific evidence that castration is an effective cure for violent sexual behavior; and (ii) there may be less harsh alternative cures such as drug therapies available. Considering the severity of castration, its use would not be justified at this time.

Ethical

There are no recommendations or laws that rapists should be castrated in Judaic, Islamic, Buddhist, or Christian literature. Castration seems to be more of a modern cry for revenge against rapists than an ancient precept. The Ethical Editor knows of no religious group which espouses castration as punishment for rape today.

In Islam, black slaves were castrated and used as servants in harems. Castration did not prevent them from having amorous but non-procreative relationships with women.

Castration is not mentioned as a practice by Jewish, Islamic, Buddhist, or Christian writers. However, in early Christian history, Origen (185-254 AD) took literally the Gospel's word about making an eunuch of oneself for the Kingdom of God's sake. (Matt. 19:12) He castrated himself, although he lived to regret doing so.

Psychological

Historically, some boy singers were castrated not for punishment but to preserve the quality of their voices into manhood, and some male slave guards were castrated to shield the females of Moslem harems from unwanted pregnancy; this practice also existed in China, and has continued into this century.

However, castration has been a punishment for male sexual offenders, especially rapists, in various cultures and localities for centuries, presumably on the theory that since eunuchs are gentle folk, rapists would become gentle and non-violent following castration. However, eunuchs were castrated before puberty, before male secondary sex characteristics developed, and before they had experienced sexual intercourse. Mortality is said to have been 20 to 25%.

A 1981 study in West Germany indicated that among adult rapists who had voluntarily agreed to castration, sexual desire and arousability, frequency of coitus, sexual thoughts and masturbation were reduced but not eliminated. Almost a third were able to engage in sexual intercourse. In general, it was not proved that castration removes the psychological hatred that motivates the rapist and the results of the study did not seem to justify castration of rapists.

27   PROOF OF RAPE

Legal

If forcible rape is charged, the state must prove beyond a reasonable doubt that defendant had sexual intercourse with his victim and that the intercourse was without her consent.

Penetration, however slight, must be proven; ejaculation need not have occurred but the presence of semen as by emission can provide evidence of penetration.

Under current law, a victim need not physically resist the rape to indicate that she does not consent to the contact; rather, her verbal resistance is sufficient. Obviously, proof of lack of the victim's consent is not a problem if it can be established that she was unconscious, drugged, or mentally incompetent at the time of the intercourse. Two special consent issues may make it difficult to obtain a rape conviction. One is that some victims may not raise any verbal resistance because of fear that their aggressor will become physically violent. In such case, the victim's lack of consent can still be established if a jury determines that her fear of bodily injury was reasonable. Second, even if it is established that the victim did not consent, the state must be prepared to counter a claim by a defendant that he reasonably believed that his victim was willing to have sexual intercourse.

Defendant's belief that consent was given may be a special problem in acquaintance rape cases, particularly if defendant and his victim had previous consensual relations. There are two traditional rules of evidence that have also made some rape convictions difficult to obtain. The first is that a defendant cannot be convicted on the uncorroborated testimony of his victim. The second is that evidence of the victim's past sexual conduct with persons other than the defendant may be introduced at trial. Evidence of past sexual behavior is helpful in casting doubt on a victim's claim that intercourse with the defendant was nonconsensual. Both of these evidentiary rules are abandoned by most jurisdictions today because they unfairly place barriers to rape convictions that are not present for other crimes. However, evidence of a victim's past relations with the defendant is still admissible if defendant is claiming that he reasonably believed that his victim consented to the act for which he is charged.

If statutory rape is charged, the state need only prove that defendant in fact had intercourse with the victim and that she was under the age of legal consent at the time.

Psychological

Rape is so degrading and humiliating to victims their feelings of shame often interfere with reporting the crimes. Medical and legal examinations following a rape are still, in some jurisdictions, so demeaning and harassing that victims prefer to avoid reporting the crimes.

28 FALSE ACCUSATION

Legal

False accusations may be brought concerning sex crimes, including child sexual abuse, as for any other crimes.

Accusations may be more difficult to refute in the area of sex crimes, however, since such crimes typically occur in private with the participants the only witnesses and often there is no physical evidence. It amounts to one person's word against another person's denial; the complainant may be a child, even a quite young child.

If an adult totally without any basis in fact accused another of a sex crime, such an accusation itself would be actionable by the person accused against the accuser. However, if the accuser had some grounds for making the accusation, even if such grounds proved to be too weak to support a conviction, the accusation itself would most likely not be actionable.

Because of the gravity of sex crimes, especially if the victim is a minor, the law will always take accusations of sex crimes very seriously.

Psychological

It is not true that females make frequent false accusations of rape; however, occasionally, motivated by anger, or seeking revenge, or trying to protect themselves from some other kind of accusation, they may falsely accuse.

29   FORNICATION

Medical

There are no medical aspects of fornication, other than the increased medical risk of contracting a disease or of creating an unwanted pregnancy.

Legal

Fornication in the criminal law means sexual intercourse between two unmarried persons. In the past it was a crime in almost all jurisdictions. Now the majority of jurisdictions do not penalize consensual sexual intercourse between adults in private. These states will punish a person for fornication only if there is force or the victim does not consent (see 24 RAPE), if the victim is below the prescribed age (see 25 STATUTORY RAPE), or the act is done where the public might view it.

Many states continue to make fornication a crime, however, although the penalties often are reduced and the crime is a misdemeanor rather than a felony.

Ethical

In Judaism fornication is referred to twice in the Old Testament—Genesis 38:24 and Deuteronomy 22:21. Both references refer to a woman "playing the harlot." In both cases fornication is severely condemned. Genesis 38:24 explains the "sin" of Tamar. Her father-in-law, Judah, without knowing that it was his daughter-in-law, had mistaken her for a harlot, had sex with her, and she conceived by him. When he discovered the wrong he had done her, he interceded for her and protected her from punishment. She gave birth to twins!

Deuteronomy 22:21 asserts that the woman found without the tokens of virginity, ostensibly at the time of a possible marriage, has been "playing the harlot" and shall be stoned to death.

In Islam, the Koran exacts severe punishment for fornication, for both men and women. It says: "Scourge each of them with a hundred stripes, let no pity affect you in regard to them." (Sales Translation, Ch. 24, p. 343)

In Buddhism, fornication is prohibited. See 16 PROSTITUTION-ETHICAL.

In Christian literature, the Apostle Paul says: "Be sure of this, that no fornicator or impure man, or one who is covetous (that is, an idolater), has any inheritance in the kingdom of Christ and of God." Fornication was condemned because it was so closely associated with idolatrous practices of people in the Hellenic world. Furthermore, it is also rejected today; it is often called promiscuity rather that fornication. Promiscuity, especially since the appearance of sexually transmitted diseases such as syphilis and AIDS, is heavily condemned. See 7 PROMISCUITY-ETHICAL.

Psychological

In today's outspoken society, constant media attention to the pleasures of intercourse (with virtually no attention to the risks and responsibilities), or peer pressure, or simple curiosity, may compel some to try it although their values warn not so to do; the resulting tension can produce feelings of guilt or anxiety. Still others engage in unmarried sex with pleasure and without shame or guilt.

30 ADULTERY

Medical

There are no medical aspects of adultery, other than the increased medical risk of contracting a disease or of creating an unwanted pregnancy.

Legal

Adultery is a crime in which two persons not married to each other engage in sexual intercourse while one or both of the participants are married to others. Like fornication (see 29 FORNICATION), adultery has been decriminalized by the majority of states, unless it is accomplished by force or against the will of the victim, the victim is under the prescribed age, or the act occurs in public. Many states, however, do make adultery a crime and penalties vary greatly, from several months imprisonment to years (five or ten, maybe more).

There was a time when in some states, notably New York, adultery was the only ground for divorce. In states which employ fault grounds for divorce, adultery continues to be one of the grounds for divorce.

Some states retain a civil action for criminal conversation, in which the spouse whose husband or wife has committed adultery may sue the person with whom the adultery is committed for damages. It is sufficient to prove the adultery to establish a basis for the awarding of damages, whose amount rests with the discretion of the court. There may also be liability if the jurisdiction retains action for alienation of affections, an action brought by the injured spouse against the one who alienated the affection of such spouse's husband or wife. Again damages are determined in the discretion of the court.

Ethical

In Judaism, Jewish law strictly prohibits adultery. (Exodus 20:14, Leviticus 18:20, Deuteronomy 5:18 and 22:22) Adultery was seen primarily as the violation of a husband's right to have sole possession of his wife and to have assurance that his children were his own. The penalties for adultery were the stoning of both the woman and the man. In contemporary American Judaism, the matter of an extramarital affair would be dealt with in a compassionate but confrontive way in rabbinical counseling. Learning from the experience to strengthen the marriage would be primary.

Adultery is prohibited in Islam. True believers are urged to keep themselves from "carnal knowledge except for their wives." (Koran, Sales Translation, Ch. 23, p. 335) A partner who accuses a spouse of adultery is required to bring proof to the ecclesiastical judge. Women have the right to prove that their husbands are liars if the husbands cannot prove that the wives are adulteresses. In each such case, the judge can urge that the man and woman separate permanently: "...but though the woman does swear her innocence yet the marriage is void, or ought to be declared void by the judge because it is not fit that they should continue together after they have come to such extremities."

Islamic nations that attempt to follow strict orthodoxy continue to apply stoning for adultery, even though such regulations are not in the Koran but in the Traditions which are of uneven authenticity.

In Buddhism, adultery cuts across at least three of the Five Precepts. See 1 ABSTINENCE-ETHICAL. It is a form of "taking what is not given," a sexual misconduct, and a form of deception of one's spouse. The more moral and virtuous the person transgressed against, the more serious the offense.

In Christian teachings, Jesus moves the discussion of adultery from the mere overt act to the intentions of the heart of the adulterers. (Matthew 5:27-30) In dealing directly with adulteresses (in his day contrary to Jewish law, adultery was a woman's sin and not a man's also) Jesus dealt compassionately and in a forgiving way toward adulteresses. (John 4:7-42 and 8:3-11) He pointed them to a high vocation for their lives, and told them to go and sin no more.

Today religious groups universally disapprove of adultery. Principal among such groups are the Roman Catholic Church and orthodox Protestants. However, among more liberal Jewish, Catholic, and Protestant groups, the leadership is also concerned with the lessons that can be learned from an adulterous affair, relative to impairments of the marriage.

Psychological

Adultery is committed for many psychological reasons: boredom, neglect, revenge, lust, infatuation, excitement, or love.

Responses vary according to individual differences and individual situations, but the adulterer may well suffer a troubled conscience with feelings of guilt and anxiety.

Adultery is usually committed in secrecy; fear of being found out can heighten marital tensions.

The abandoned or "cheated" spouse may experience anger, depression, shame, and even guilt if blame is assumed for the spouse's adulterous behavior.

CONCEPTION

Who's Affected

Females can conceive, that is, become pregnant, between puberty and menopause.

Puberty is the age at which a female or male becomes capable of reproduction; the law generally presumes that age to be 12 for a female and 14 for a male.

Menopause is the change that takes place in a female, usually between 45 and 50 years of age, when menstruation (see below) and the capacity for conceiving a child (that is, conception) ceases.

Pregnancy is a period of gestation; that is, the time between conception and childbirth, during which the child-to-be develops in the uterus.

Consultation

When planning to become pregnant, a female should seek the advice of a physician, following a thorough physical examination. Pregnancy involves major changes in almost all parts of a female's body; and the physician can help insure that such changes will occur in a normal and healthy manner, minimizing the chance of an unanticipated disorder. Pregnancy, however, is a serious circumstance for a female involving some risk of toxicity (eclampsia) and, infrequently, death. Before becoming pregnant, a female should be tested to determine whether she is immune to infection from the rubella (German measles) virus.

Cause

Pregnancy begins when a female's mature ovum (egg) is penetrated by a male sperm cell; such penetration is called fertilization, or conception. See THE BEGINNING OF HUMAN REPRODUCTION, opposite. Conception normally occurs as a result of sexual intercourse; it can only occur during five days of the female's menstrual cycle.

Menstrual Cycle

A female is able to become pregnant periodically, and the sequence of events connected with these periods is called the menstrual cycle. The cycle lasts 28 days on the average, and is best envisioned as a regular thickening and subsequent sluffing off of the uterine lining, together with other events.

The cycle is controlled by a system of interrelated hormones or other chemicals, and influenced by nutrition and disease.

During days one through ten, following the end of menstrual discharge and beginning the cycle anew, the uterine lining becomes ready to receive a fertilized ovum, or egg. About the eleventh day, an ovum is released from an ovary, and begins its journey down one of the two Fallopian tubes to the uterus. This trip takes about five days, from days 11 through 15. The ovum is capable of being fertilized during these five days, and after day 15 becomes inert.

If the ovum is not fertilized, it resides in the uterus for seven to nine days. The prepared lining of the uterus is not needed. Hence, it and the unfertilized, inert egg are shed during the four days that are days 25 through 28. This shedding, which is called "menstruation" involves the discharge from the body of the thickened, blood-filled lining of the uterus via the vagina; the 28-day span is called the menstrual period.

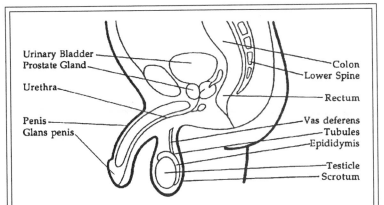

Urinary Bladder
Prostate Gland
Urethra
Penis
Glans penis

Colon
Lower Spine
Rectum
Vas deferens
Tubules
Epididymis
Testicle
Scrotum

The Beginning of Human Reproduction

Male sperm is produced in the testes, and excreted through small tubules, the epididymis, vas deferens (duct), and the larger urethra.

In sexual intercourse, the sperm is ejaculated into the female's vagina. From the vagina, it works its way through the cervix into the cavity of the uterus and through the uterus into the Fallopian tubes. In one of the tubes, it fertilizes an ovum, which is an egg produced in the ovary. The fertilized egg moves into the uterus and embeds itself in the lining of the uterus. Pregnancy has begun.

If the fertilized egg develops outside the uterus, it is an ectopic pregnancy; if it develops in one of the Fallopian tubes, it is a tubal pregnancy. Both of these conditions present major risk to the female, and usually require surgical intervention.

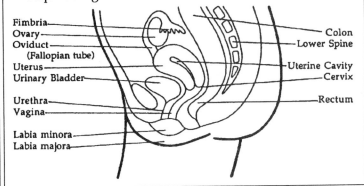

Fimbria
Ovary
Oviduct
(Fallopian tube)
Uterus
Urinary Bladder
Urethra
Vagina
Labia minora
Labia majora

Colon
Lower Spine
Uterine Cavity
Cervix
Rectum

Figured another way, the 28-day period may be broken into the 14 days from ovulation until the onset of menstruation, and the 14 days to complete menstruation and to prepare the uterine lining anew.

If the ovum is fertilized, it is by a single one of millions of sperm placed in the vagina by sexual intercourse, or by artificial insemination. This swarm of sperm normally works its way from the vagina through the cervix and uterine cavity into the Fallopian tubes, and usually encounters the ovum in one of the Fallopian tubes.

Sperm can live up to six days in the uterine environment. Thus, sexual intercourse (or artificial insemination) which takes place five days before ovulation or five days after ovulation can result in conception. That is to say, sperm placed in the vagina from day six through day 15 can cause conception.

When an ovum is fertilized, it embeds itself in the uterine lining, and the many complex steps of pregnancy begin.

Achievement

Most couples achieve conception with relative ease, by sexual intercourse; such couples are called fertile. However, about one-sixth of all couples capable of pro-creation cannot readily achieve conception; if, after a year of trying, they still fail to do so by intercourse, they are considered to be infertile. See 31 INFERTILITY. Depending upon the diagnosis of the cause of infertility, a physician might advise an infertile couple still wanting a child of their own, but not by adoption, to try artificial insemination, various techniques of in vitro fertilization, or surrogacy.

Artificial insemination involves placing the sperm in the vagina by instrument rather than by intercourse. See 32 ARTIFICIAL INSEMI-NATION.

Surrogacy involves fertilizing the ovum of one female in vitro, and placing the resultant embryo in the uterus of another female, the surrogate. See 33 IN VITRO FERTILIZATION; also see 34 SURROGACY.

Avoidance

A couple wishing to create a pregnancy has the best chance of success if sexual intercourse occurs during ovulation and the six days before, or approximately days six through 15 of the menstrual cycle, described above.

However, for those who wish to avoid pregnancy, the only certain ways before menopause are refraining from sexual intercourse or by sterilization of one of the two partners. See 35 VASECTOMY; also see 36 TUBAL LIGATION. Contrary to juvenile notions, sexual intercourse the first time may well result in pregnancy. So may intercourse under water, or standing up, or with the use of contraceptives, particularly inexperienced use.

If normal sexual intercourse is practiced, there are numerous ways of lessening the chances of pregnancy; but none is absolutely reliable.

The withdrawal method depends (see 37 WITHDRAWAL METHOD) upon the male's removal of his penis from the vagina before ejaculation and the assumption that no living sperm are in the prostatic secretions which are emitted before the ejaculation.

The rhythm method depends on the usual situation that a female can become pregnant only during days approximately 11 through 15 in her menstrual cycle. During these days, she must refrain from intercourse; or she or her sexual partner must rely on contraceptives. The rhythm method depends (see 38 RHYTHM METHOD) upon successful prediction of the ovulation period. The prediction can be attempted by:

The basal body temperature method, which depends upon noting a rise of 0.5 of a degree Fahrenheit in a female's body temperature at ovulation (this is best done using a special thermometer with an extended scale); or

The calendar method, which depends on determining a female's personal ovulation period by timing six or more of her menstrual cycles; or

The mucus inspection method, which depends on analysis by observation of the changes in cervical mucus to determine the ovulation period.

Many couples do not use the above two birth control methods, but do use contraception. See 39 CONTRACEPTION.

There are several mechanical methods of contraception which make use of diaphragms, cervical caps, condoms, and IUDs (intrauterine devices) to lessen the chance of becoming pregnant. Diaphragms, cervical caps, and condoms all attempt to block the passage of sperm from the vagina into the uterus. How IUDs work is not precisely known, but it is thought that they interfere with the uterus's ability to accept a fertilized ovum. See 40 MECHANICAL METHODS.

There are several chemical methods of contraception. These include spermicidal creams or jellies and contraceptive foams, tablets, and suppositories. These, too, lessen the chance of conception. Spermicides contain chemicals such as nonoxynol-9 intended to kill sperm on contact. Foams, tablets, and suppositories depend upon trapping sperm in bubbles. See 41 CHEMICAL METHODS.

Some of the mechanical and chemical devices are well used together; for example, a diaphragm with spermicidal jelly.

Finally, birth control pills, (see 42 PILLS) which interfere with female hormone levels and thereby prevent ova from maturing and being released, are effective in lowering the chances of becoming pregnant.

For a comparison of the relative effectiveness of various contraceptive methods see 43 CONTRACEPTIVE FAILURES.

There are other contraceptive methods widely practiced in Europe, but not approved by the FDA for use in the U.S., including injections and implants. However, in late 1990, the FDA did approve a long-acting contraceptive implant for use by females. By a minor surgical procedure, under local anesthetic and in a physician's office or at a clinic, six small rods are placed under the skin. The rods contain a hormone trade named Norplant, and generically known as levonorgestrel; the hormone is released slowly over a period of five years. This contraceptive implant is said to be 99% effective in females of average weight.

Confidential contraception advice and materials are offered by Planned Parenthood, a national organization with local affiliates in many U.S. cities; the local offices are listed in telephone directories. Some affiliates also provide counseling about infertility and abortion, and, less often, abortion services.

Many local health departments also offer contraception advice and materials as part of family planning clinics; these, too, may be found listed in telephone directories.

Although it is not a contraceptive and is not approved by the FDA for use in the U.S., RU 486 is in use by many French females to terminate pregnancy by a private, self-induced abortion. See ABORTION, page 183.

Symptoms

Early symptoms of pregnancy include: missing a period after having been regular; having a short, scanty period; having tender, swollen breasts with darkened nipples; feeling nauseated for no readily apparent reason; urinating more frequently; having an increased vaginal discharge; feeling abnormally tired; or suddenly losing interest in some foods previously liked.

Diagnosis

If pregnancy is suspected, it can and should be confirmed by a physician. In an advanced stage, the physician can often diagnose pregnancy by a pelvic examination. In the very early stages, however, a urine test for pregnancy is necessary for diagnosis. Such a test can be obtained from a physician, a family planning clinic, or a commercial pregnancy-testing service; or a test can be self-administered by use of a kit bought from a drug store. A physician should confirm the diagnosis.

Risks

Despite its essential and frequent occurrence, pregnancy involves a number of major and minor risks to mother and the developing child. A number of diseases contracted by the mother may be passed to the unborn while in the uterus or during delivery. An inadequate diet for the mother may result in abnormal developments in the unborn. Drug abuse on the part of the mother will harm the developing child. If the mother smokes, delivery may be premature. And there are many physical changes which occur to the mother's body during pregnancy which if incorrectly attended may result in harm and/or discomfort to the mother, and harm to the baby-to-be.

Treatment

If the pregnancy and a baby are wanted, the procedures to be followed during a successful pregnancy are described in FULL TERM PREGNANCY, page 155.

If the pregnancy is unwanted, decisions, sometimes painful, are inevitable. Matters for consideration are suggested under UNWANTED PREGNANCY, page 167.

---

31 INFERTILITY
Medical

Male infertility sometimes results from inability to deliver sperm into the vagina because, for example, of impotence. See 4 IMPOTENCE.

However, the most common causes are low sperm count or sperm defects. Low sperm count can result from the use of alcohol, tobacco, or drugs; or even from underwear so tight that it raises the temperature of the testes to reduce sperm production. Sperm defects can result from damage to or blockage of sperm-carrying tubes, caused by diseases such as gonorrhea; or by damaged or abnormal testes.

Female infertility sometimes results from failure to ovulate. Such a failure is often caused for no readily apparent reason, but can be caused by stress, hormone imbalance, or impairment of the ovaries.

Other causes of female infertility include: blockage of sperm from entering the Fallopian tubes (such blockage can result, for example, from pelvic inflammatory disease) and a uterine disorder, such as endometriosis.

In some cases, the female's cervical mucus is such that it kills her partner's sperm, thus to cause infertility.

Approximately half of all professionally treated infertile couples eventually achieve conception.

Legal

The infertility of a spouse is not itself a ground for having a marriage declared void. However, if a person intentionally conceals before marriage the fact that he or she is infertile, his or her spouse may be able to have the marriage declared void on the ground of fraud. A woman who becomes infertile as a consequence of a venereal disease may be able to recover damages from the transmitter of the disease in a civil suit. Treatment for infertility is often costly. It should be noted that health insurance policies commonly do not cover the cost of infertility treatment. See 20 HEALTH INSURANCE.

Ethical

The Old Testament Scriptures, which are held sacred by Judaism, Islam, and Christianity, have much to say about infertility. In brief, the teachings are that God is the giver of children, that prayer is the main force that uninhibits a woman from becoming pregnant, and that her anger, frustration, and complaint about infertility can be poured out positively to God in prayer. In the Old Testament, there are several cases of infertility mentioned. In Genesis 18:1-15, messengers of God or God himself assured Abraham at the Oaks of Mamre that Isaac would be born to him and Sarah. In I Samuel 1:9-19, Hannah is assured in her prayers and in conversation with Eli, the priest, that she would have a child; she gave birth to Samuel. In Judges

13 the wife of Manoah—her name is not given—was assured by messengers from God of the birth of Samson.

Judaism, Islam, and Christianity share these stories, which reflect the confidence of their adherents in the effectual power of prayer in the face of infertility. To the secular mind, this may seem naive, but the Scriptures are saying that total surrender of a couple's whole being to the sovereignty of God in their lives releases them from the idolatry of having a child. When relaxed in repose, a couple is more apt to beget. A modern clinical example of this is a post-adoptive pregnancy, which occurs after a couple has given up on the expectation of having a child, adopts, relaxes, and then conceives.

For Christianity, in the New Testament, the message is repeated. In Luke 1:8-39, Zechariah and Elizabeth are said to have conceived in their old age and to have parented John the Baptist upon the promise of God.

Psychological

Infertility can produce feelings of frustration, inadequacy, and doubts of self-worth in couples, especially if family or social pressure, expressed or implied, emphasize having children as desirable and dutiful. In some cases, the couple may blame each other for the failure to conceive, and see the problem as interpersonal instead of medical or psychological.

32   ARTIFICIAL INSEMINATION
Medical

Artificial insemination has been utilized for many years, usually by infertile couples who, even after treatment for infertility, cannot achieve conception by intercourse; but sometimes by single females who want single parenthood.

Insemination usually takes place in specialized clinics where semen is injected by instrument into the cervix during the period when conception is most likely; the procedure can be repeated monthly if necessary, but usually not longer than six months. An artificial insemination procedure costs about $250 to $350 per try.

If the husband can be the father, his fresh semen, produced by masturbation, is used. If the semen must be that of a donor, usually anonymous, it is withdrawn from a frozen storage bank. Semen from the husband and from the bank is sometimes mixed; in this case identity of the father is not known.

To reduce the risk of disease transmission by semen, a donor's semen is first tested for certain microbes such as the one causing syphilis; and then it is held before banking until the donor himself has been tested free from diseases such as AIDS and hepatitis B. However, even after such tests there is a risk that some infectious agent not tested for in the semen or donor, will transmit disease.

Sperm banks do not offer a selection of semen known to be genetically compatible with the female's genes; such banks do offer a racial selection of semen.

Legal

Many states have enacted laws that govern the legal status of children conceived by artificial insemination. Under these laws, a child conceived from the sperm of an anonymous donor is deemed to be the natural child of its mother's husband provided the husband consented to the procedure. Some statutes go further and provide specifically that the donor shall have no parental rights or obligations toward the child. If a married woman is inseminated without the consent of her husband or if a state does not have laws governing the procedure, the child could be deemed illegitimate and the husband may not be liable for its support, although if he has assumed a parental role, a court may find that he must support the child under principles of equity. It is not clear in these latter situations whether the donor may assert parental rights to his biological child.

Many physicians performing artificial insemination will not accommodate requests for insemination from unmarried women. A woman in this position may choose to inseminate herself with sperm donated by an acquaintance. In at least one such case, a court granted visitation rights to the donor father on the theory that it is in the best interests of a child that he be nurtured by both a mother and father whenever possible.

If a woman contracts a venereal disease from infected sperm, she may have a cause of action in negligence against the physician, sperm bank, and possibly the donor involved in the insemination process. See 19 DAMAGES. It should be noted that some sperm banks do not medically screen their donors for the existence of genetic diseases. Therefore, a child conceived from the sperm of an anonymous donor may face unknown health risks.

Ethical

The sacred writings of Judaism, Islam, Buddhism, and Christianity have nothing specific to say about artificial insemination.

Contemporary teachings are specific in the official Catholic prohibition against artificial insemination, especially if with semen from a donor, as a breach of the sacramental union of husband and wife. This view is based on the belief that marriage is "marriage in Christ," which symbolizes the "marriage of Christ and his Church." The marital relationship is believed to be formed before God and by God and no one is to put this sacred bond "asunder," i.e. to intervene between husband and wife. Artificial insemination is seen as breaching this holy bond, and therefore as an adulteration of the marriage. A single woman outside the sacred bond of marriage using artificial insemination would be considered as engaging in fornication. (See *Catholicism*, Richard McBrien, [Minneapolis: Winston Press, 1981], 1015-1026.)

This same view is held by some conservative Episcopalians, and by many less liturgical but highly fundamentalist Protestants, but without specific official church statements.

Jewish and Islamic teachings are much more liberal with respect to artificial insemination, as indeed are liberal Protestant teachings. The scientific capability can be interpreted as one of God's gifts because infertility is against God's will, and the birth of a child to wanting parents is a fulfillment of God's will.

Buddhist teachings can be inferred to mean that infertility and parentlessness can interfere with the eight-fold path from ignorance to knowledge and from suffering to Nirvana. Artificial insemination ostensibly could remove this hindrance.

Psychological

Artificial insemination ideally should involve some psychological preparation on the part of the couple undertaking it. Some religious backgrounds might have warned against it. A couple might have some concern about genetic defects in the donor's semen. Assuming a couple would undertake artificial insemination only after unsuccessful infertility therapy, prolonged attempts might heighten frustration, and lead to stronger negative feelings such as mentioned in 31 INFERTILITY.

Thorough counseling beforehand should enable most couples to recognize their fears and concerns, and should enable them to balance these negatives against the positives of the prospect of becoming parents.

A single female considering artificial insemination should be certain she understands the obligations and demands of single parenthood, else she may come to see her child as a misfortune if she is overwhelmed by the task.

So far as is known, semen donors have no psychological consequences from having so done.

33 IN VITRO FERTILIZATION

Medical

In vitro (in glass) fertilization is fertilization of a female's ovum by the male sperm, accomplished in a highly specialized clinic rather than in vivo, that is, in the living female. For development into a normal embryo, the fertilized ovum can be returned to the female who created it, or it can be transferred to a surrogate. See 34 SURROGACY.

Although in vitro fertilization is not widely practiced, it is accomplished somewhere every day; but only about one attempt in ten is successful. The complicated process costs between $6,000 and $8,000, and takes about two weeks from induction of ovulation to uterine implantation.

Miscarriage rates are slightly higher following in vitro fertilization, and multiple births occur more frequently when this procedure is used.

Legal

Currently, there are few legal barriers to a couple conceiving a child by in vitro fertilization using the husband's or a donor's sperm and the mother's ova. It is frequently assumed that the holding of the United States Supreme Court concerning privacy in Roe v. Wade protects this form of procreation. Legitimacy of the child could be an issue if a donor's sperm is used without the husband's consent. See 32 ARTIFICIAL INSEMINATION.

Troubling legal issues may arise when embryos created by in vitro fertilization are "orphaned" or rejected by the individuals who contributed to their creation. It is becoming common to freeze excess embryos for use in the future. After freezing, one or both of the prospective parents may die or the couple may divorce, raising questions as to the status of the embryos.

In a New Zealand case, an American couple who were the biological "parents" of frozen embryos died in a plane crash. A New Zealand court was faced with the dilemma of deciding the proper disposition of the embryos. It eventually held that the embryos could be implanted into the womb of a woman who was not the biological mother of the embryos; however, if a child was born subsequently, he would not be considered to be the child of the deceased couple for inheritance purposes.

Recently, a divorcing couple in Tennessee disputed "ownership" of frozen embryos. The wife sought custody of the embryos so that she could conceive a child after the divorce; her husband claimed ownership of the embryos as marital property. He further maintained that if his wife were to conceive a child with the embryos he should not be held to the obligation of a parent because that child would have been conceived without his consent. A Tennessee appellate court granted custody of the embryos to the wife. It refused to characterize the embryos as property that could be destroyed at the convenience of its owner. The court further refused to exempt the husband from parental obligations for any child subsequently born, preferring to defer that issue to a time when the controversy actually existed.

In anticipation of problems such as those above, it is common for an in vitro fertilization clinic to require couples to sign a contract giving to the clinic the right to destroy embryos in the event of the death or divorce of the couple. Given the sensitive issues involved in the possible characterization of embryos as "persons," it is quite possible that such contractual provisions would be unenforceable.

Ethical
The official Catholic view of in vitro fertilization is similar to the official view of artificial insemination, and for the same reasons; and the same things said of artificial insemination concerning Jewish, Islamic, Buddhist, and liberal Protestant teachings can be said of in vitro fertilization if the procedure is between husband and wife. See 32 ARTIFICIAL INSEMINATION.

The critical question of ethics is what to do with the fertilized conceptus that may remain after an in vitro procedure? Are fertilized ova persons? If so, to toss them out is abortion; or to use them with someone other than the parents is a form of adultery.

Psychological
The psychological aspects of in vitro fertilization are most likely similar to those involved in artificial insemination. See 32 ARTIFICIAL INSEMINATION.

34 SURROGACY

Medical

In surrogate parenthood, an ovum from one female is fertilized in vitro (see 33 IN VITRO FERTILIZATION), and the resulting fertilized ovum is placed in the uterus of another female, the surrogate, who carries the fetus to term. An infant carried by the surrogate may be the genetic child of:

—a husband and a wife;

—a husband and an ovum donor, not his wife;

—a sperm donor, not her husband, and a wife;

—a sperm donor, not her husband, and an ovum donor, not his wife.

The traditional roles of motherhood are divided by surrogacy; the genetic mother who contributes the ovum, the birth mother who carries the fetus, and the social mother who raises the child may be three different persons. Most cases to date have involved the surrogate's assumption of the middle role of birth mother, and for the genetic mother to be the social mother.

The role of fatherhood may be genetic, social, or both.

For a couple intending to have a child by surrogacy, the services of the genetic father and the birthing mother may be provided free, or by contract for money.

Legal

Surrogacy raises a variety of legal issues, few of which can be resolved with any certitude. The term itself is applied to different situations.

In the famous Baby M case from New Jersey, the media referred to the birth mother as a surrogate mother because she had contracted with a married couple to be artificially inseminated with the husband's semen, to become pregnant, to carry the child to term, and then voluntarily to relinquish her parental rights so that the genetic father and his wife could adopt the baby. That was not a situation of surrogacy, but of artificial insemination (see 32 ARTIFICIAL INSEMINATION), in which the genetic and birth mother was the "real" mother and the child had no biological or legal relationship to the sperm donor's wife. Although a lower court recognized the contract and would order the birth mother to turn over the child for adoption, the Supreme Court of New Jersey held that the contract was unenforceable.

The genetic parents would be treated as any other parents of a child born out of wedlock: one would have physical custody and the other would have visitation.

In a later case where a wife's ovum was artificially inseminated in vitro and the result was inserted into the uterus of a woman who had contracted to carry it until birth, the court ruled that the child was the child of the genetic parents and the birth mother could not refuse to turn the child over to its genetic parents; here the contract was enforceable.

Very few states have any legislation concerning surrogacy.

Many refuse to enact laws allowing surrogacy because such a procedure appears to be too close to buying and selling children, which is always and everywhere forbidden. The exchange of money with respect to the gestation and birth of a child appears to be commerce in babies. Some also think it could be a procedure in which poor and uneducated women would be financially pressured into carrying children for wealthy women who did not want the burden of pregnancy.

On the other hand, surrogacy may provide a method by which infertile couples could have a child which is genetically the child of one or both of them.

From a legal perspective, surrogacy is a terribly risky procedure. The process of artificial insemination or in vitro fertilization is expensive; the expenses of the woman who is carrying the child will be great, as are the costs of childbirth. There is probably no guarantee that the woman who has carried the child will not change her mind after the baby is born and decide to raise her child herself. There is great probability the court will allow her to do so.

The strongest case for surrogacy would be made by two persons who are the genetic parents of the child. Even here, however, courts may not be willing to overturn the classical notion that the woman who carries and gives birth to the child is the child's legal mother. If that happens, the husband who donated the sperm would remain the legal father with the obligations of paternity. See 49 PATERNITY; see also 52 SUPPORT.

Ethical

Nothing explicit appears in the ancient sacred writings of Judaism, Islam, Buddhism, and Christianity about surrogacy by in vitro fertilization; the technology of surrogacy is recent. There is, however, an Old Testament story (Genesis 16:1-15) that could serve as an example of surrogate parenthood, namely the story of Abraham, who at his wife's request and blessed by God, fathering a baby by Hagar, Sarah's handmaiden.

Based on the teachings discussed under artificial insemination (see 32 ARTIFICIAL INSEMINATION), there are in general two modern views of surrogacy by Christians. Official Catholic teaching considers the marriage bond a sacramental bond not to be violated by the entry of another woman into the dyad in any manner; hence surrogacy is condemned as adultery, and a "sundering" of the sacred relationship between husband and wife.

The other view is held by those who consider marriage not a sacrament, but as a teaching and learning relationship between husband and wife; the covenant between the couple accepts surrogacy as a new revelation of the possibility of becoming parents of their own biological child. Those who hold this view see redemption and hope in the new technology when it is taken with thanksgiving in prayer to God, and the process would be a religious covenant before God between the married couple and the surrogate. If accomplished without payment (except for specific obstetrical and pediatric costs), liberal Christians might see the surrogate's act as one of spiritual generosity by one woman for another and her husband, in the covenant of faith all three share together. The consecration and spiritual relationship of the three could make surrogacy a way of exploring new reaches of the grace of God.

This latter view will be taken or not taken by Jews on an continuum depending on their adherence to Orthodox or Conservative or Reformed Judaism.

At this writing, no teachings of Islam and Buddhism on surrogacy are to be found; one might expect Islamic and Buddhist views to be similar to their views on artificial insemination.

All religious groups would very likely condemn the commercialization of surrogacy motherhood as the possible creation of a "slave breeder class" of women.

Psychological

The couple attempting to gain a child to raise by surrogate motherhood quite literally enters into a psychological triangle; whereas between the couple there was one relationship, with the surrogate there will be three relationships. Little work has been done to study such situations, their evolutions, and their outcomes. The Psychological Editor believes the effects will be complicated, and deeply felt, and will be even more so after the birth of the child and as it grows.

35 VASECTOMY

Medical

Vasectomy is a sterilization procedure whereby the male vas deferens is divided by surgery to keep sperm from reaching the penis, thus to prevent its transmission to the female in sexual intercourse. The purpose of a vasectomy is to avoid pregnancies, while continuing to have otherwise normal sexual intercourse. The only material removed from the semen is the spermatozoa; seminal fluid from the prostate gland is still present in the ejaculate. A male with a vasectomy can still perform and enjoy sexual intercourse.

Vasectomies are not immediately effective. Some sperm remain in the vas deferens beyond the surgical division; and until these are ejaculated or die, the male is fertile. The male must have two successive semen specimens tested sperm-free before he is considered sterile; this testing usually takes two to four months after the operation. During such time, he and his partner should use a contraceptive method to reduce the chance of having an unwanted pregnancy, or abstain.

The operation, usually performed by an urologist, can be done as an out-patient. The cost is approximately $500 to $700.

The operation is only sometimes reversible; the success rate is less than 40%.

Legal

The decision of a competent adult to be sexually sterilized for nontherapeutic purposes is protected as one aspect of a general right of privacy in making procreative decisions. This right of privacy is derived from the federal constitution and frequently from individual state constitutions as well. Thus, neither the federal government nor a state government can impose significant barriers to sexual sterilization without demonstrating a compelling interest for doing so.

Reasonable regulation of surgical sterilization as a medical procedure is permissible on the theory that the state has a legitimate interest in protecting the health and welfare of its citizens. Some states impose additional limitations on nontherapeutic sterilizations, which may include requirements that the person seeking to be sterilized be over the age of 21, request the procedure in writing, obtain the consent of his spouse, and his physician provide to him a full and reasonable explanation of the procedure and consult with another physician before performing the procedure. A mandatory waiting period between the patient's giving his consent and performance of the procedure may also be imposed. It is questionable, however, whether some of these requirements are constitutional in view of the United States Supreme Court's invalidation of similar requirements for abortions. See 62 ABORTIONS.

A controversial issue involving sexual sterilization is whether the state can compel a person to submit to a sterilization procedure without his or her consent. At the turn of the century, over thirty states enacted eugenic sterilization laws which enabled the states to order the sexual sterilization of persons deemed to be genetically inferior. These laws were justified on the ground that bad genes cause undesirable social and criminal behavior. The Supreme Court of the United States held Virginia's sterilization statute constitutional in 1927. Since that time, we have learned that much of the medical science underlying the claims of sterilization advocates was inaccurate. Additionally, the constitutional status of an individual's right to make decisions relating to procreation has been recognized in a number of Supreme Court decisions rendered after 1927. As a result, almost all state legislatures have repealed their compulsory sterilization statutes.

Nevertheless, there appears to be a growing sentiment today that compulsory sterilization may be appropriate in instances where individuals reproduce without regard to the health and welfare of their offspring. The indigent are particular targets of this current concern. For more on compulsory sterilization, see 36 TUBAL LIGATION; see also 43 CONTRACEPTIVE FAILURES.

Ethical

Judaism, Islam and Buddhism have no teachings or prohibitions against vasectomies. As in main line Protestantism, a vasectomy is left up to the individual in the privacy of his relation to God, his wife, and his physician.

A vasectomy is a result of very recent technology when compared with thousands of years of tradition in the major religions. The only pertinent religious teaching about vasectomies is the Roman Catholic declaration that all artificial means of contraception are sinful—a position held also by many Protestant groups. The main reason for this taboo against contraception is that it interferes with procreation, and is "unnatural."

A vasectomy is a very private act between the individual and his physician. The major penalty suffered is a private sense of guilt, if any, for having disobeyed the preachment of the church. See 26 CASTRATION-ETHICAL.

Psychological

Although both libido and potency are unaffected by vasectomy, some males who have had a vasectomy may have difficulty with erection and ejaculation, especially if they incorrectly regard the operation as castration.

When more children would be disadvantageous to a couple, vasectomy can provide a sense of security and enhance the enjoyment of coitus; but vasectomy can become a source of distress if later the couple wants more children, or the male remarries into a child-wanting relationship.

Pre-existing sexual difficulties and hypochondria have been shown to increase psychological problems for couples. A strong reason for not having a vasectomy is disagreement with the female about having it. The wife or "significant other" of a male who contemplates vasectomy may react disapprovingly or angrily if she does not concur prior to the decision.

36   TUBAL LIGATION
Medical

Tubal ligation is a sterilization procedure whereby the female Fallopian tubes are blocked by clips, or by suturing, cutting, or cauterization. The purpose of tubal ligation is to prevent sperm from fertilizing an ovum, that is to prevent conception, while continuing to have otherwise normal sexual relations. A female with a tubal ligation can still perform and enjoy sexual intercourse.

Tubal ligations are effective in preventing conception immediately.

The operation is usually performed by a gynecologist. The cost is approximately $500 to $700. The patient will have a sore abdomen for several days following the operation; any procedure necessitates entry into the peritoneal cavity by a small incision.

The operation is only sometimes reversible; reversals are successful in about 40% to 50% of attempts.

Legal

The law governing the availability and legal implications of a tubal ligation (tying of the Fallopian tubes) or a salpingectomy (cutting of the Fallopian tubes) is the same as for a vasectomy. See 35 VASECTOMY.

There are some special concerns raised with surgical sterilization procedures performed on women. A great deal of recent attention has been paid to the issue of fetal abuse. A woman may have a history of having given birth to more than one child who is impaired because of its mother's use of drugs or alcohol during pregnancy. See 45 FETAL ABUSE. There is some sentiment that she should be sexually sterilized to prevent her from harming more children during future pregnancies, given her demonstrated inability or unwillingness to control her addictive behavior.

Involuntary sterilization has also been suggested as appropriate for both men and women who have been convicted of child abuse, again on the theory that their documented history of abusing children justifies depriving them of the ability to bear and rear new victims for future abuse.

The sterilization of mentally incompetent women is also a troublesome issue. The guardian of a mental incompetent may petition a court for authorization to have the ward sterilized, claiming that the procedure is in the best interests of the ward. In many instances the incompetent is educable or trainable and would gain greater physical freedom if supervision to prevent unwanted pregnancies is not necessary. These sterilizations are neither voluntary, because the incompetent is incapable of giving her consent, nor compelled, because the incompetent has not refused to be sterilized. Ever since the rejection of eugenic theory popular at the turn of the century, courts are particularly wary of permitting such procedures. In the absence of a statute, courts are divided on the resolution of this issue, with some finding that they are powerless to authorize the procedure. In those states that permit the sterilization of incompetents, a person petitioning for the procedure must demonstrate that the interests of the incompetent would best be served by rendering her infertile. In a few states, the inability of a woman to rear a child is a relevant factor to consider in this determination. See 43 CONTRACEPTIVE FAILURES.

Ethical

The same thing can be said of tubal ligation as has been said about vasectomy. See 35 VASECTOMY-ETHICAL.

Psychological

There is a remarkably low percentage of adverse psychological effects for females following tubal ligations. On the contrary, following the operation, a sense of security and relief from fear of an unwanted pregnancy will, if anything, increase sexual enjoyment. Only occasionally, diminished libido and depressed sexual arousal will occur; this is particularly the case if the operation was not strictly voluntary but was required because of economic conditions, or other reasons.

37 WITHDRAWAL METHOD

Medical

The purpose of the withdrawal method of contraception is to prevent sperm from entering the female's vagina, thus to avoid pregnancy, while continuing otherwise normal sexual relations.

The only advantage of the withdrawal method of contraception is that it avoids the expense and inconvenience of other methods of contraception; for example, one does not have to purchase and put in place a condom. The disadvantage, besides frustration, is that the method is not reliable; with sexual arousal, there is a leakage of sperm through the urethra, so that prior to withdrawal before orgasm, spermatozoa can, and often do, reach the vagina.

See 43 CONTRACEPTIVE FAILURES.

Ethical

Islam, Buddhism, Judaism, and Christianity have no specific teachings about the withdrawal method of contraception except insofar as Islam, Judaism, and Christianity may be aware of and informed by the Old Testament story of Onan.

The withdrawal method of birth control is mentioned in the Old Testament. Genesis 38:9 states that Onan was commanded to raise up children to his brother's wife; but when he "went into his brother's wife, he spilled the semen on the ground, lest he should give offspring to his brother. And what he did was displeasing to the Lord, and he slew him also." From this story, misinterpretations of Onan's act as masturbation have persisted. The critical issue was that he refused to produce children.

Onan's method of contraception is condemned along with other methods of contraception by Catholic and some Judaic and Protestant teachings. Liberal churches and synagogues would not see the withdrawal method of contraception as a sin, but rather as producing irritability and tension between a married couple. Family counseling would discourage the withdrawal method in marriage and would suggest instead a method of contraception that enables both partners to complete intercourse in orgasm.

Psychological

Withdrawal as a contraceptive method requires alertness, strong motivation, and a high degree of physical and emotional control. It may be frustrating to the female if she fails to reach orgasm. Sexual satisfaction may be reduced for both partners because they must focus on performance rather than pleasure; the spontaneity of coitus is decidedly lessened. However, the withdrawal method is widely used.

38   RHYTHM METHOD
Medical

The intention of the rhythm method of contraception, or birth control, is to avoid the injection of the male sperm during the times of the menstrual cycle when the sperm may find and fertilize the female ovum, while continuing otherwise normal sexual relations.

The rhythm method is a medically acceptable method of birth control for a female who can always measure her menstrual cycles accurately and who is motivated to observe the days when she must avoid intercourse.

The advantage of the rhythm method is that it avoids other methods such as pills, diaphragms, or condoms. However, the female must determine with certainty when it is safe, and when it is not; the disadvantage of the method is that such a determination can easily be illusory; for example she may ovulate later in her cycle than calculated. Also, she may find it vexing to repress sexual arousal on days that are not safe.

See 43 CONTRACEPTIVE FAILURES.

Ethical

The rhythm method is the old term for that particular method of birth control; "natural family planning" is the term now more generally used.

Islam would leave the matter of birth control to the prayers and conscience of each individual couple. Buddhism would see no problem with the rhythm method unless deception is employed between man and woman. Judaism would judge the method as to its effectiveness and not as a moral or ethical issue; most Christian groups would agree.

Natural family planning methods of birth control are taught and approved by the Catholic Church and some Protestant groups. The methods are seen as "natural" rather than artificial methods of birth control. The most widely used technique is the calendar method, whereby an attempt is made to determine the woman's personal ovulation rhythm. But pregnancy rates are high, ranging from 14.4 to 47 per 100 woman-years, mainly because most couples fail to abstain for the relatively long periods required. The basal body temperature method and the mucus inspection method are also approved. "Each of these requires a great deal of motivation as well as training; in most reports pregnancy rates are relatively high..." (*New England Journal of Medicine*, March 23, 1989, p. 778) Couples are highly approved of by the Catholic Church and some Protestant groups for using such methods of birth control, which are actively taught in some private schools and approved in sermons while all other forms of birth control are discouraged.

See 43 CONTRACEPTIVE FAILURES.

Psychological

The rhythm method of contraception requires couples to abstain during the female's fertile days, or to use alternative contraception methods.

Psychologically, fear of pregnancy may lead to anxiety.

Couples may feel vexing pressure to have intercourse on unfertile days whether "in the mood" or not.

The rhythm method is only practical within a committed relationship; but despite its limitations, most committed couples using rhythm do not experience serious psychosexual problems.

39 CONTRACEPTION

Medical

The purpose of all methods of contraception is to minimize the chance of unwanted pregnancies, while continuing otherwise normal sexual relations.

Contraceptive advice can and should be obtained from obstetricians, or from gynecologists, family planning practitioners, or health department clinics. The cost of such advice is that of the medical visit; clinical visits are often free.

The costs of the methods vary. All oral contraceptives cost approximately $16 per month; a diaphragm costs approximately $40; and the insertion of an intrauterine device (IUD) is approximately $200 but is good for a three year period. Condoms cost between $5 and $7 per dozen, on the average.

Competent advice should be obtained before adopting for use any contraceptive method.

See 43 CONTRACEPTIVE FAILURES.

Legal

Because the decision not to procreate is constitutionally protected, a state cannot prohibit the distribution of contraceptives to adults. However, in many states, a minor may not be able to obtain a prescription for contraceptives without the consent of a parent. Minors have relatively easy access to non-prescription contraceptives such as condoms (even if it is not legal to sell them to minors), and may have access to those that must be medically prescribed through a sympathetic physician.

At the moment, there is no general type of contraceptive drug or device that is prohibited by law. If current abortion law changes, however, states may choose to designate fertilization as the moment when life begins and afford protection to fertilized ova on the theory that they are "persons." In this event, contraceptives such as IUDs that prevent the implantation of a fertilized ovum may be prohibited.

Many contraceptives, such as the pill or an IUD, pose health risks to the user. The manufacturers of these drugs or devices as well as the physicians who prescribe them could be held liable to users for injuries to their health. Liability may also arise from allegations that a contraceptive used while a woman was pregnant has harmed her child. This was the case in a recent multimillion dollar verdict awarded against a manufacturer of a spermicidal jelly.

Ethical

Judaism's attitude toward specific artificial methods of birth control is somewhat exemplified by the approval, in 1935, of the Conservative Rabbinical Assembly. However, the approval preceded the Holocaust. Whereas Jews do not legislate against birth control, they nevertheless strongly encourage the replenishment of their people, six million of their kinspersons having been destroyed during the Holocaust.

Islam legalized birth control in 1961. A decrease in the birth rate seems to have followed the effects of education and urbanization. Probably the biggest factor producing the increase in the use of birth control, is the entry of women into the workplace. It is reported that more than two thirds of salaried Islamic women of child-bearing age use contraceptives.

In Buddhism in America, it seems, contraception does not violate any of the Five Precepts (see 1 ABSTINENCE-ETHICAL) unless deception in the use of, or the failure to use, contraceptive measures comes between husband and wife. Deception would transgress the rule: To abstain from false speech.

Christians are divided in their attitudes toward and teachings of contraception. In 1930, the Lambeth Conference of the Anglican Church of England approved artificial contraception, as did the Federal Council of Churches in 1931. Other Protestant groups leave contraception to the spiritual discretion of their followers.

However, in the Catholic Church, Pope Pius XI, who was the Pope during the nineteen thirties and forties, issued the encyclical *Casti Cunubi* which banned all methods of birth control except abstinence during the woman's fertile times. Pope Paul VI, in 1966, after the discovery of the oral contraceptive, issued his encyclical *Humanae Vitae* in which he ruled that the use of artificial contraception is morally wrong.

Other factors in addition to ethical issues affect the decision of a couple whether or not to use birth control measures. Such factors include: under population, such as the Jews after the Holocaust, and the Iranians after their bloody, ten year war; over population as in China; the entry of women into the work force creating the "two pay check family"; and the conscious decision of a couple not to have children for a variety of other personal reasons.

Psychological

Few sexually active teenage girls make use of contraception regularly for various reasons; a common reason is the feeling that preparing for intercourse with contraception means they are "bad" whereas spontaneous, unprepared activity is "good." Another reason for not using contraception stems from the girls' fear of getting caught by having the contraceptive devices or substances found by disapproving parents.

It has been shown that some teenage males believe that sex without their use of condoms demonstrates love.

When couples disagree over the method of contraception, or over who should be responsible, psychological sexual problems may be created for them.

Contraceptive methods that are not reliable are, psychologically, anxiety-producing. See 43 CONTRACEPTIVE FAILURES.

The advice of King K. Holmes, et al., in *Sexually Transmitted Diseases*, 2nd Ed. (New York: McGraw-Hill, 1990), on page 82, to prevent the transmission of STDs applies as well to prevent unwanted pregnancies: "Teenagers should be encouraged to use barrier contraceptives, especially both condom and vaginal spermicide, with every coital act, whether or not the female is using the oral contraceptive."

The sexually active female who disapproves of contraceptives, perhaps because of religious convictions, has a difficult judgment to make: which is the greater risk to her mental and physical health, the use of a contraceptive, or an unwanted pregnancy if no contraceptive is used?

Evidence from other cultures indicates that knowledgeable adolescent sexual relationships that are not coercive and are not opposed by the cultures do not produce harmful psychological effects if effective contraception is used. In our own culture, such concerns as out-of-wedlock pregnancy, venereal disease, and family and societal disapproval remain extremely relevant.

40   MECHANICAL METHODS

Medical

Mechanical methods of contraception include the diaphragm, the cervical cap, the condom, and the intrauterine device (IUD); the purpose of all such methods is to prevent unwanted pregnancies, while continuing otherwise normal sexual relations.

The purpose of the first three devices is to block the male sperm from the female vagina or uterus. The IUD is thought to prevent the fertilized ovum from attaching to the uterine lining.

The diaphragm and cervical cap are excellent methods of contraception providing they are properly fitted by a physician and are used effectively and consistently. The advantages are that they are not hormonal, and are totally under the control of the female. They need to be carefully inserted prior to intercourse and left in place for at least six hours thereafter. The disadvantages of the diaphragm and cervical cap are that the female may not use them properly; that they may sometimes fall out of the vagina; and that they need to be inserted prior to each engagement, which may be regarded as being a nuisance.

The condom is also an excellent contraceptive device. The advantages are that it is not hormonal; it is readily purchasable, is totally under the control of the male, and in addition to protecting against conception, it also protects against disease. The disadvantages, besides expense, are that some persons may be allergic to latex condoms, and there is always the possibility of the condom's rupture.

The medical risk of an intrauterine device depends on the individual. The female receiving the IUD should have had pregnancies in the past and not have had a history of pelvic inflammatory disease. Past medical difficulties with the IUD may have resulted from poor selection of females for IUD use. The IUD must be prescribed and fitted by a physician.

See 43 CONTRACEPTIVE FAILURES.

41   CHEMICAL METHODS

Medical

The aim of chemical methods of contraception is to deprive sperm of their ability to fertilize the female ovum, by killing or trapping, while continuing otherwise normal sexual relations.

Any chemical method depends upon the effective installation of a material such as a spermicidal jelly, in the vagina. Such materials are available over the counter. A spermicide may be contained in a sponge, which is placed in the vagina to emit the spermicidal substance. If not on a sponge, the material must be placed directly in the vagina.

The advantage is that chemical method material is available in pharmacies throughout the country. The disadvantage is that it is not a reliable method. For example, the material may not be put in place long enough prior to intercourse to be dispersed throughout the vagina. The possible negative side effects include an allergy; or a perceived increase in a vaginitis, as the material can run out of the vagina.

See 43 CONTRACEPTIVE FAILURES.

42   PILLS

Medical

The purpose of oral contraceptive pills is to prevent the female ova from developing and being released into the Fallopian tubes, while continuing otherwise normal sexual relations.

Such pills, which must be prescribed by a physician, are exceptionally reliable; they are the most effective method of contraception. The physician will advise who may, and who should not, rely on contraceptive pills.

The advantages of oral contraceptives are that they are easy to take; they cause minimal change in the female; they allow spontaneous sex since nothing needs to be done in preparation for intercourse; and failures are few. The disadvantages are that they should not be taken by females who have high blood pressure; females who have a history of hormonal cancer; or by females who cannot tolerate the pill but develop nausea and vomiting. Also they may, and occasionally have resulted in a stroke or thrombophlebitis; but this generally occurs only in smokers.

Numerous commonly prescribed medications can negate the effectiveness of contraceptive pills. Among interfering medications are: antibiotics, such as rifampin, chloramphenicol, ampicillin, penicillin, sulfonamides, nitrofurantoin, neomycin, and isoniazid; anticonvulsants, such as primidone, phenytoin (trademarked Dilantin), phenobarbital, and ethosuximide (trademarked Zarontin); and a third group including phenylbutazone, meprobamate, cyclophosphamide, chloropromazine, phenacetin, and chlordiazepoxide.

To avoid taking an interfering medication, a female relying on an oral contraceptive should not take any other medication concurrently with the pill without the approval of her physician.

See 43 CONTRACEPTIVE FAILURES.

43   CONTRACEPTIVE FAILURES
Medical

The failure experience of couples using various methods of contraception has been studied by the medical profession, with illuminating results.

The study determined that if 100 young, healthy couples use the pill method of contraception to prevent unwanted pregnancies, for one year, there will very likely be only one or two failures among them. Or if they use the pill for ten years, there will likely be only ten to twenty failures, or for 20 years, 20 to 40 failures, among them.

In contrast, if the 100 couples use the rhythm method for one year, there will likely be 20 failures among them. Or if they use rhythm for ten years, there will likely be 200 failures, or for 20 years, 400 failures, among them.

Relatively speaking, the rhythm method is about ten to twenty times more likely to fail than the pill method.

Of course, the experience of each couple in the group may vary from the average. To illustrate, failures among the 100 couples mentioned above, using rhythm for 20 years, will likely average four failures per couple; however, one couple may use rhythm without a single failure while another will have eight failures, to make four the average for the two couples.

There are two important conclusions to be drawn from experience:

- For a single couple the rhythm method can be effective in beating the average, but is quite risky compared to the pill method;
- For large groups rhythm is certain to be, comparatively, a relatively ineffective means of birth control.

Finally, contraceptive failure rates are compared:

100 COUPLES—ONE YEAR

The method of conception used for one year by a group of 100 sexually active young couples	The number of unwanted pregnancies, or "failures," to be expected in the group, in one year
Pill	1-2
IUD	3-4
Condom plus spermicide	5-6
Diaphragm plus spermicide	5-6
Condom alone	15
Diaphragm or cervical cap alone	15
Rhythm	20
Spermicide alone	25
No contraception or "birth control"	90

Adapted from a chart in the American Medical Association's *Encyclopedia of Medicine* (New York: Random House, 1989), 304.

Legal

A manufacturer or provider of contraceptives will not be liable to a user for the failure of the drug or device to prevent a pregnancy if the user was properly instructed about how to use the product and was warned that the product may not be 100% effective. Liability could arise from the negligent manufacture of devices or drugs.

To date, legal problems arising from the effectiveness of contraception relate primarily to a conception that occurs after the negligent performance of a sexual sterilization operation.

A legal action complaining about the birth of an unwanted child is called a wrongful pregnancy or wrongful conception suit. Almost all courts that have heard such suits are willing to award plaintiffs damages to compensate them for the costs and suffering of an unwanted pregnancy; however they are unwilling as a rule to compensate plaintiffs for the expenses of rearing the initially unwanted child to its majority. Courts reason that as a matter of law, a healthy child cannot be a legal injury to its parents. There are some courts, however, that will award damages for rearing expenses, provided that the damages are reduced by a financial assessment of the the benefits experienced by plaintiffs from parenthood.

FULL TERM PREGNANCY

Prenatal Planning and Care

Mothers-to-be, traditionally, have been concerned during pregnancy to protect the health of the babies-to-be, as well their own health. Now, however, the legislatures and the courts have undertaken an active interest in protecting the rights of the fetus. It is asserted, for example, that the fetus has a right to be born free from genetic disease. See 44 WRONGFUL LIFE-WRONGFUL BIRTH. It also has a right to be born free from injuries caused by its mother's neglect or abuse. See 45 FETAL ABUSE.

Thus, morally and legally, once the physician has confirmed a welcome pregnancy, it is of major importance to prescribe, and for the mother to observe, a program of prenatal care to protect the health of the mother and of the child-to-be.

A normal pregnancy is divided, medically and legally, into three trimesters (that is, three periods of roughly three months each); and each trimester has its own characteristics. However, there are considerations normal for all three trimesters, as follows:

Diet is extremely important because what the mother eats nourishes the developing baby. A balanced diet prescribed by a physician should be strictly followed.

Alcohol and other drugs (see 46 DRUGS) may harm the baby-to-be and should be avoided. A pregnant female should never take any drugs (including over-the-counter drugs) or go on any special diet without first consulting her physician.

155

Nicotine from smoking is known to cause the baby to be underweight at birth; and to increase the risk of premature delivery.

Medications should not be taken, unless prescribed by the physician.

Exercise should be maintained unless the physician advises against it.

Travel should be undertaken only if approved by the physician; and medical records should always be taken if travel is unavoidable, especially if the travel is abroad. (Airlines will not take females during the last weeks of pregnancy because of the risk of delivery during the flight.)

Intercourse up to the sixth month of pregnancy is safe. Later it may cause early labor and delivery.

Nausea, commonly known as morning sickness, occurs in about half of all pregnancies during the first three months.

Heartburn, which is caused by the stomach contents re-entering the esophagus and irritating its lining, is common during pregnancy.

Anemia, if it develops, may increase the chance of a premature baby. In the event its symptoms appear (paleness, weakness, tiredness, shortness of breath, fainting and palpitations), the physician should be contacted promptly.

Constipation is common, but no laxative should be taken without the physician's advice.

Frequent urination is caused by compression of the bladder by the growing fetus.

Loss of sleep is not unusual, but no drug or sedative should be taken unless prescribed.

Backache occurs because the spine comes under strain as a result of the shifting center of balance; but may be somewhat alleviated by using legs to lift while not bending the back; and by prenatal exercise.

Blood pressure fluctuates normally, sometimes due to anxiety. High blood pressure must be discovered early and monitored by the physician. Very high blood pressure may be associated with a toxic pregnancy and require a Cesarean section to protect the health of both mother and child.

First Trimester (Weeks 0-12±)

For the first eight weeks of pregnancy, the baby-to-be is called an embryo; for the last 32 weeks, it is called a fetus.

In the first three months, tissues and organs are rapidly organized and developed, and especially vulnerable. Any infection the mother might contract can cause damage; also, any drug reaction can harm the developing infant to be.

Two major first trimester complications are miscarriage and ectopic pregnancy.

A miscarriage, medically known as a spontaneous abortion, is said to occur when a pregnancy ends spontaneously before the twentieth week. After the twentieth week, a spontaneous end is known as stillbirth if the baby is born dead, and as premature delivery if the baby is born live. If the pregnancy is ended electively, the end is known as abortion, and medically is called termination of pregnancy.

Miscarriages occur when the placenta with the developing embryo or fetus inside separates from the uterine wall. Such miscarriages usually happen during the first fourteen weeks of pregnancy, although the terminology extends until the twentieth week.

The cause of the separation is often unknown, but some abnormality is usually present. Miscarriages from falls and accidents are rare.

There are four kinds of miscarriages; and the physician should be consulted promptly when symptoms occur:

Threatened miscarriage: Symptoms are cramping and discomfort, accompanied by vaginal bleeding, sometimes preceded by a brownish discharge.

Inevitable miscarriage: Symptoms are pain in the lower abdomen accompanied by the expulsion of a dead embryo or fetus.

Incomplete miscarriage: Pain and bleeding are the same as an inevitable miscarriage; but the dead embryo or fetus has not been wholly expelled.

Missed miscarriage: Disturbances are wholly absent, except the symptoms of early pregnancy disappear; and the dead embryo or fetus must be removed by a physician.

Miscarriages of any kind are emotionally upsetting, and can lead to depression.

More than six months should elapse before conception is attempted again for the best outcome of a subsequent pregnancy. See 47 CONCEPTION.

A disorder with symptoms similar to but more intense than those of a miscarriage is an ectopic pregnancy.

Ectopic pregnancy: Symptoms are increasingly severe abdominal pain, particularly during the first trimester. Symptoms may be confused not only with those of a miscarriage, but also those of appendicitis, or an infection of the Fallopian tubes. Vaginal bleeding is common. An ectopic pregnancy, the result of a fertilized egg lodging outside the uterus, requires urgent surgical correction.

Second Trimester (Weeks 13-27±)

Many females say that during the weeks of the second trimester they have never felt better. The rate of fetal growth has slowed, and so the nutritional demands on the mother's body have lessened. Amniocentesis, a fetal diagnostic procedure, may be performed between the sixteenth and eighteenth weeks of pregnancy. See 48 FETAL MONITORING.

The principal medical problems of this time are incompetent cervix and hydramnios. A physician should be consulted promptly when the following symptoms occur:

Incompetent cervix: Symptoms are those of an inevitable miscarriage; the cervix has opened allowing the fetus and placenta to escape from the uterus, which in turn leads to the miscarriage.

Hydramnios (excessive fluid around the baby): Symptoms may be none; or sometimes shortness of breath, indigestion, and abdominal tightness; or, rarely, a sudden onset of swelling.

Third Trimester (Weeks 28-38±)

Generally, babies are healthier if born at full term. Treatment to accomplish full term includes rest and prescribed drugs to relax the uterine muscles. Sometimes a physician will conclude that the baby has a better chance of survival outside the uterus, and will induce labor or perform a Cesarean section.

Among medical problems that are unlikely but may occur in the third trimester are pre-eclampsia, eclampsia, antepartum hemorrhage, placenta previa, intrauterine death and retarded fetal growth. If a symptom occurs, the physician should be seen promptly.

Pre-eclampsia: Symptoms are headaches, blurred vision, intolerance of bright light, and also nausea; vomiting and salt and water retention may occur. A major danger of pre-eclampsia is its progression to hypertension and full eclampsia.

Eclampsia: Symptoms are convulsions and sometimes unconsciousness. Eclampsia risks the lives of the fetus and of the mother, but can be treated.

Antepartum hemorrhage: This refers to any vaginal bleeding after the twentieth week. Such bleeding may result from a broken varicose vein, cervical damage, separation of the placenta from the uterine wall or placenta previa.

Placenta previa: Symptoms may be non-existent. However, there is usually sporadic to heavy painless vaginal bleeding resulting from a low-lying placenta in the uterus. If the bleeding becomes a hemorrhage, an immediate Cesarean delivery will be necessary to protect the mother's life.

Intrauterine death (the death of the baby in the uterus after the twentieth week): Symptoms are the cessation of movements by the un-born baby. While the cause of death may be pre-eclampsia, eclampsia, hemorrhage or an abnormal baby, often the cause is unknown.

Retarded fetal growth: Symptoms may be non-existent. The retardation may result from an inadequate placenta. The risk to the baby is inadequate growth and possible death in utero. Periodic prenatal testing by the physician is required to monitor fetal well being.

Childbirth

The birth is complete after the baby is delivered and the placenta is discharged from the uterus. The entire process is called labor, and occurs in three stages:

Dilation of the opening of the cervix and contraction of the muscular uterine wall;

Expulsion of the baby; and

Afterbirth when the placenta is discharged.

At the onset of labor, the membranes that surround the baby rupture, and release the amniotic fluid. This is natural and is known as breaking water.

From time to time, the membranes will rupture prematurely, before labor has begun, and in this event the physician will prescribe proper treatment.

Postmaturity

The symptom of postmaturity is delayed labor or the start of labor long after the baby is mature or due. The risk to the baby is brain damage or even death; however, upon prompt diagnosis, birth may be induced, or accomplished by Cesarean section, with reduced risk to the baby.

Incidence

In 1988, an estimated 3,913,000 live births occurred in the United States; about 21% were births by unmarried females.

---

44   WRONGFUL LIFE-WRONGFUL BIRTH

Legal

A health care practitioner's negligence in delivering genetic counseling to prospective parents or in failing to diagnose an impairment in a fetus may give rise to a wrongful birth and wrongful life claim.

Both actions involve a child who was born with birth defects. Parents allege in a wrongful birth action that they are injured by giving birth to a child whose conception or birth they would have chosen to avoid if they had been informed of the child's condition. A wrongful life claim is brought on behalf of the impaired child, who alleges that but for the negligence of the defendant, he or she would not have been born into a life of pain and suffering. The essence of the claim is that the child's defects are so severe that it would have been better if he or she had never been born at all. Most courts refuse to recognize wrongful life claims. They premise their refusal on adherence to a basic cultural precept that life is precious; therefore, they cannot find that non-life is preferable to life. Additionally, they reason that even if it is conceded that a person can be injured by his own life, the injury is non-compensable because the determination of damages requires an impossible comparison of the value of non-life over an impaired life.

Notwithstanding these difficulties, the supreme courts of California, New Jersey, and Washington have recognized the validity of wrongful life claims. These courts acknowledge the sensitive issues raised in plaintiffs' claims, but choose to focus instead on the fact that because defendant was negligent, a child exists who suffers and has special needs.

Recently, an intermediate appellate court sitting in Indiana recognized a wrongful life claim arising from the negative circumstances surrounding plaintiff's birth. The infant's parents were both patients at a private residential facility for the mentally and physically impaired. The plaintiff was conceived when his mentally ill father raped his profoundly retarded mother. The plaintiff alleged that the operator of the facility was negligent in supervising his parents. The Indiana court held that a life such as the plaintiff's was wrongful under circumstances where parents are incapable of deciding to have and care for a child.

Unlike wrongful life claims, almost all courts that have heard wrongful birth claims recognize their validity. Courts characterize the alleged injury in a wrongful birth claim as being the deprivation by the defendant's negligence of the plaintiff's right to accept or reject the parental relationship. Successful plaintiffs are able to recover damages to compensate them for the special medical and educational expenses to be incurred because of their child's impairment, the same type of damages recoverable by a child in a successful wrongful life claim. In some states, damages for the pain and suffering parents experience in raising an impaired child are also compensable.

Clearly, both of these causes of action raise sensitive and disturbing issues: whether courts are willing to recognize an injury based on the deprivation of an opportunity to have an abortion, and whether courts are willing to assess the value of an infant's life. Such cases have been controversial since their inception. Accordingly, some legislatures have responded by enacting laws that prohibit one or both of these claims.

45   FETAL ABUSE

Legal

Pregnant women who act without regard for the welfare of their unborn children may be subject to legal sanction.

In numerous recent cases, mothers who have given birth to drug-exposed infants have been charged under criminal abuse and neglect laws or laws prohibiting the distribution of controlled substances to minors. Most of these laws describe the victim of the criminal act as a "child" or a "minor," both terms traditionally interpreted to mean a person who has been born alive. For this reason, a number of attempted prosecutions have failed because the statute under which the defendant was charged is held not to be intended to protect the unborn. The State of Florida recently avoided this problem by successfully arguing that defendant, who had used cocaine during her pregnancy, had delivered a cocaine derivative to her child, a born person, through the umbilical cord for the sixty to ninety second period between the birth of her infant and before the cord was clamped.

Prenatal substance abuse has also been a ground for terminating a woman's parental rights to her child after its birth in a civil neglect proceeding. In these cases, a child born suffering the effects of exposure to illegal drugs or alcohol is held as a matter of law to be a neglected child.

Women, even those who have not used controlled substances during pregnancy, may find themselves interfacing with the legal system. Pregnant women who refuse to heed the advice of their physicians may be compelled by court order to submit to unwanted medical procedures. There are numerous recent instances in which women have been ordered to submit to Cesarean sections or blood transfusions deemed necessary to save the life of their viable fetuses. Courts have reasoned in these cases that the state's interest in the life of a viable fetus justifies what is held to be a relatively minimal intrusion into the autonomy interest of the mother.

Ethical

In the case of a father who abuses an unborn fetus by abusing the pregnant mother physically and/or sexually, Judaism, Islam, Buddhism, and Christianity would all agree upon criminal punishment for the father. In the case of the pregnant mother who carelessly abuses her unborn child by using alcohol and/or drugs, the adherents of all four religious faiths would probably support legal measures against the mother with mandatory drug abuse treatment as part of the penalty. If a pregnant mother knowingly risks passing, and in fact passes a venereal disease or drug addiction to her child, the function of any American religion would be to bring forgiveness for any sense of sin the mother feels, and to restore her to a right relationship with God, with a spirit of gentleness.

Psychological

If the mother understands how she has harmed the fetus, and if she is able to experience normal emotions, she likely will suffer remorse, guilt, and depression.

If she raises the child herself and therefore becomes fully and daily aware of the handicaps she produced, these emotions normally will be intensified; however, paradoxically, the handicapped child may be burdensome and arouse her anger and such a child may in turn be abused.

46   DRUGS

Medical

A pregnant female's use of alcohol may retard the growth of the fetus, and may result in serious defects including mental retardation. It is not known what amount of alcohol consumption will affect the fetus; therefore, no consumption at all during pregnancy is safest.

Nicotine increases carbon monoxide to the fetus and decreases growth; the average newborn of a mother who is a smoker weighs about half a pound less than the newborn of a non-smoker.

Cocaine is even more dangerous; it causes intense vasospasms, or tightening of the arteries, which prevent blood flow in the placenta or in the fetus. Prevention of blood flow in the fetus's brain causes such deterioration that the newborn will have either cerebral palsy, or significant motor or learning disabilities. Other narcotics such as heroin and PCP, also have intense destructive effects on the placenta, on fetal blood flow and directly on fetal tissue.

Legal

See 45 FETAL ABUSE.

47   CONCEPTION

Medical

It has been shown that after a miscarriage a subsequent pregnancy will be more successful if sufficient time is allowed to elapse; a minimum of six months is recommended by the Medical Editors.

Psychological

Following a miscarriage, the psychological consequences are highly variable. One might be relieved to have miscarried;

another might feel guilty if she believes some act of hers caused the spontaneous abortion; yet another might be depressed if the baby lost was much wanted.

If depression is suspected, a careful history and physical examination may be needed to diagnose the type of depression and to determine the treatment indicated; psychotherapy, possibly with antidepressant medication, is usually the therapy for depression.

48   FETAL MONITORING

Medical

Analysis of the amniotic fluid that surrounds the fetus can detect some fetal abnormalities such as chromosomal abnormality, sex-linked disorders, metabolic diseases (such as Tay-Sachs disease), and some developmental disorders (such as spina bifida). The sex of the fetus can be determined by chromosome analysis.

Fetal monitoring is not always recommended; the age of the pregnant female and family history are considerations.

Legal

See 44 WRONGFUL LIFE-WRONGFUL BIRTH.

Ethical

Today parents can determine during pregnancy whether their child-to-be will be so severely handicapped, mentally and/or physically, that it will have little or no chance in life; for example, an anencephalic child, i.e., a child without a brain. Parents can gain such information early in the pregnancy thanks to sonogram monitoring and chromosomal study of the genetic composition of the unborn fetus by means of amniocentesis.

The purpose of such medical procedures is to inform the parents. When they learn of such an abnormality, the parents have the options of having the pregnancy interrupted by medical means or continuing to term. Sometimes the fetus will spontaneously abort or miscarry; but if medical abortion is necessary, the ethical concerns about abortion must be resolved before a decision is made. See 62 ABORTIONS-ETHICAL.

The Ethical Editor cannot find Islamic data regarding fetal monitoring, and invites information from readers.

Jewish teachings do not prohibit such fetal monitoring; on the contrary, many Jewish researchers and practitioners have been active in encouraging monitoring; they are particularly concerned because, as an ethnic group, Ashkenazi Jewish children are subject to the Tay-Sachs disorder.

Nothing the Ethical Editor has been able to find in the Buddhist codes of morality is opposed to fetal monitoring.

In Christianity, persons opposed to interrupting a pregnancy would include Catholics and Protestants who are opposed to all abortion. Such persons would insist that the parents of a deformed child would be ennobled in their spiritual maturity by taking the responsibility of caring for a deformed child as long as it lives. However, some Catholics and Protestants believe that malformations of a fetus, such as the absence of a brain, justify abortion on ethical and spiritual grounds; such persons would suffer grief from the loss of their child as in the case of a miscarriage.

UNWANTED PREGNANCY

Who's Affected

The female and her life-style are affected far more drastically than the male and his life-style by an unwanted pregnancy.

In Wedlock

The problems of an unwanted but legitimate pregnancy of a wife are few compared to those of an unwed female. Unless an abortion is elected, for example, because of high physical risk of the wife's surviving childbirth, the wife and her husband may simply adjust their style of living, and prepare to enjoy their baby. Not always, however; see RELATIONSHIPS, below.

An unwanted pregnancy as a result of adultery frequently leads to divorce with wrenching emotional effects on all concerned. In divorce, it is the wife who suffers the greater financial hardship. Even though it is she who most often takes custody to raise the children alone, following divorce the husband usually will experience a substantial increase in income after expenses while the custodial mother will take a substantial decrease because of child-raising expenses, holding a low-paying job or no job at all, and/or delinquent child support payments.

Out of Wedlock

Pregnancies out of wedlock occur frequently now, and with less of their former social stigma. Nevertheless, unwanted pregnancies pose immediate problems for both sexual partners, but particularly for the female.

And not just the parents are affected. A study of infant mortality in 1983, published in 1990 by the Centers for Disease Control, found significantly higher infant mortality (death during the first year of life) for babies born to unmarried mothers. The study goes on to explain that such deaths are related to poverty; and that families headed by an unmarried mother are often likely to be living in poverty.

Anguish

Highly sophisticated blood tests can identify the father of a child with 98% accuracy. See 49 PATERNITY. Both the male and female immediately face important questions, such as:

- Should she secure an abortion?
- Should they marry?
- If full term is decided upon, who will pay the obstetrician, the hospital? See 50 EXPENSES.
- When the baby is born, who will take custody? See 51 CUSTODY. What amount of child support will the non-custodial parent provide? See 52 SUPPORT.

The mother is legally obliged to care for the child; abandoning the child could be a crime. See 53 ABANDONMENT. She may provide for the child's adoption by placing the child with a licensed child care agency or, if the state law so allows, with certain identified relatives. See 54 ADOPTION.

Neither financially able parent can escape child support. By new laws, and by old laws more strictly enforced, states are vigorously enforcing child support judgments (see 55 JUDGMENTS) by such devices as automatic wage assignments. Furthermore, to insure that such judgments are sufficient, all states now provide support charts based upon surveys of the cost of raising a child.

Of all single custodial parents, approximately 95% are female and not all court ordered child support judgments are paid in full. Unfortunately, in many cases the single custodial female finds that she must raise her child or children (wanted or unwanted) in poverty, or near poverty. She may receive no child support from an impoverished or run-away father, many have low-paying jobs (if any) and many receive less from the government's Aid to Families with Dependent Children (AFDC) than is necessary to support a family above the poverty level.

Relationships

The personal outside relationships of a married couple who have an unwanted but legitimate pregnancy are normally not affected. As between the couple, however, sometimes such a pregnancy can result in crowding and financial strain, inability to pay bills, emotional abuse, and stress.

The personal and financial relationships of the male contributor to an unwanted illicit pregnancy can be affected, but are often less affected than are the relationships of the pregnant female. If the male is married but not to the pregnant female, the changes in his marriage can be horrendous, if the pregnancy becomes known to his spouse and children. Financially, too, strains can be introduced; for example, wage assignments for support can be embarrassing and burdensome.

But the relationships of the female pregnant because of an illicit union are often strained or broken.

If she is married, how will her relationships fare with her:

- Husband?
- Parents?
- Children?
- Friends?
- Employer?
- Religious organization?

If she is an unmarried adult, how will her relationships fare with her:

- Parents?
- Siblings?
- Friends?
- Employer?
- Religious organization?

If she is a minor, how will her relationships fare with her:

- Parents?
- Siblings?
- Friends?
- School?
- Religious organization?

Incidence

There is no way to determine accurately how many pregnancies, in and out of wedlock, are unwanted.

However, births in the U.S. by unmarried females were reported by the National Center for Health Statistics to be approximately the following from June, 1987, to June, 1988:

Ages	Births	%
18-24	465,000	57.8
25-29	177,000	22.0
30-44	163,000	20.2
Total	805,000	100.0

Regarding unmarried females under 18 years of age, the latest U.S. government figures are for 1986, when an estimated 133,000 births occurred among such females.

It is reasonable to assume that a substantial number of these births by unmarried females resulted from unwanted pregnancies.

49 PATERNITY

Medical

There is a medical means of determining the father of a newborn with virtual certainty, namely by HLA (human leukocyte antigen) typing, which is a specific form of DNA (deoxyribonucleic acid) fingerprinting.

Such typing is done in medical centers where tissue typing is readily available.

The cost of HLA typing ranges from $750 to $1,000.

Legal

Paternity litigation is a legal action in which a court is asked to determine who is the legal father of an individual.

While similar litigation concerning who is an individual's mother is possible or even probable in a time of technological parenting (in vitro fertilization, surrogacy, and embryo freezing and transfers), historically there have been few "maternity" actions for the fact of pregnancy and childbirth was sufficiently public to prevent the need of litigation to determine the mother's identity.

If the mother of the child is married at the time of conception or birth of the child, her husband is presumed to be the father. In some jurisdictions, even today, that presumption cannot be rebutted except upon proof that the husband was impotent (see 4 IMPOTENCE) or away from his wife so that sexual intercourse would have been impossible at the time of conception.

If the mother is not married at the time of conception or birth of the child or if her husband has denied paternity, then a paternity action is necessary to determine who is the father. The action may be brought by the mother, by the state or whoever is supporting the child, by a guardian ad litem (one appointed temporarily for purposes of this lawsuit to represent the child), or in a few jurisdictions by the person alleging that he is the father. The court will hear proof, which is typically physical evidence. It is possible to test the blood of the mother, child and alleged father and blood tests will determine who cannot be the father. Further tests (HLA testing) can determine statistically the likelihood of any given individual's being the father. In addition to physical evidence, the court may look to testimony concerning sexual intercourse between the parties at the time of conception and other evidence concerning paternity.

If an individual is found to be the father of the child, he will have legal rights (see 56 PATERNAL RIGHTS) and duties (see

50 EXPENSES, 52 SUPPORT, 55 JUDGMENTS).

It is harder to bring paternity actions after the alleged father has died because physical evidence (blood and tissue) would no longer be available.

Under federal legislation's direction, states have now extended the statute of limitations (the time during which a paternity action may be brought) to eighteen years, the present age of majority in most states.

50   EXPENSES

Medical

A full term pregnancy attended by a physician with delivery of a healthy, normal baby in a hospital, may cost approximately $5,000. The expense of other pregnancies can be astronomical; for example, an infant born at 27 weeks who spends three months in intensive care can have a hospital bill exceeding $150,000.

Legal

If a man is found by a court to be the father of a child, the court can impose upon him some or even all of the expenses connected with the pregnancy, including the costs of prenatal care of the mother, hospital costs, physician's costs, and costs incident to pregnancy and childbirth. How much of such costs the individual will be ordered to pay will depend upon the court's finding of the person's financial condition. It may be that an unemployed person without funds is unable to pay anything at all.

A minor who is found to be the father may also be liable for expenses.

At least one state has passed a statute making parents liable for the expenses of pregnancy and childbirth for any children conceived by their unmarried minor children.

51   CUSTODY

Legal

Custody of a child means child rearing and education. By common law and in most states by statute custody of a child belongs from the time of birth to the parents, if they are married to each other at the time of the child's birth or were married to each other at the time of the child's conception. One must distinguish factual custody (day to day child care, with whom the child lives, who sees to meals, schooling, medical care, discipline) from legal custody (the person(s) recognized by law as having authority to make decisions about the child, especially the basic decisions concerning education, medical care and religion). Generally, parents married to each other have legal and factual custody.

If the mother is unwed at the time of delivery and has never been married to the child's father, she alone has custody. The father may achieve legal recognition as parent in a paternity suit. See 49 PATERNITY.

While parents have custody, they have both duties (to support the child, to provide for the child's medical care and education, to discipline the child) and rights (to the care, companionship, and earnings of the child). Because the law does not recognize except in limited circumstances (see 62 ABORTIONS) the capacity of a minor (person under 18 years of age) to make decisions, parents must make decisions and give consent for actions of their children.

If parents seriously fail to perform their duties or abuse or abandon the child, the state in its overall authority to provide for persons not able to care for themselves will provide. The state may take temporary custody by taking children in need of care into its jurisdiction or even, if parental rights are terminated, permanent custody. See 54 ADOPTION.

At the time a marriage is dissolved, if there are children of the marriage the court must determine which parent(s) will have physical and legal custody. Often one parent is given custody while the noncustodial parent pays support. Both parents may be given authority to make decisions about the child (legal custody), while the child lives most of the time with one parent (physical custody).

52   SUPPORT

Legal

At common law and by statute parents (or in their absence, legal guardians) are responsible for the support of minors (generally 18 is the age of majority but those below 18 may be emancipated by marriage or, in some places, by a legal action of emancipation).

Parents usually remain liable for the support of children over 18 who are legally incompetent (mentally retarded or mentally ill or otherwise incapable of supporting themselves).

In a few states, statutes provide that step-parents are liable for the support of stepchildren so long as the marriage endures and so long as the children are minors. In most states, however, step-parents have no legal obligation to support stepchildren.

Support includes the provision of necessities: food, clothing, shelter, medical care, and education. If the parent providing support also has legal custody (see 51 CUSTODY), that parent may choose what support to provide. If one parent has legal custody and the other pays support, then the spouse with legal custody has the right to make decisions concerning health care, religion and education.

The obligation to support a child ceases if the child dies during minority; the parent would be obligated to pay for the funeral and burial of the child.

If there is a court order providing that a parent pay for the support of a child, the death of the parent will not ordinarily terminate the obligation of support. Rather, the support obligation will fall on the deceased parent's estate. If there is no court order and a parent dies, there is usually no obligation on such parent's estate to provide for the support of minor children surviving the parent.

If the parent dies without a will, a minor child will be an heir and take a share of the estate; however, if the parent disposes of all the estate by will, there is no obligation to provide for a child. Parents may disinherit even their minor children by leaving all of their estates to others.

53 ABANDONMENT
Legal

Abandonment of a child means failure to provide for a child with the intention of not providing for it then or in the future. Mere failure to provide is not abandonment if the failure is caused by illness, poverty, or other situation in which it is not possible for the parent to provide for the child. Abandonment does not sever the legal relationship between parent and child. If a parent abandons a child, the legal obligation to provide remains and a court can order the parent to care for and support the child. If there is continuing refusal to provide, the court may order support by attaching the parent's property or garnishing the parent's wages. A parent is not free to walk away from a child and claim no further obligation to the child.

Abandonment may provide a justification, however, for the state to terminate the parental rights of the abandoning parent. If the state proves by clear and convincing evidence that the parent has abandoned the child, the state may terminate that parent's parental rights and place the child with the other parent or in a foster home or state institution for needy children.

Cases in which abandonment is a factor are difficult to decide because it is often difficult to determine whether there was an abandonment or simply a failure to provide for some period of time because of special circumstances like illness or poverty.

Some courts have found that a parent who is imprisoned upon conviction for a crime has abandoned a child, for the voluntary commission of the crime has as a foreseeable consequence the likelihood that the parent may be imprisoned and thus incapable of caring for the child. The abandonment could then constitute grounds for terminating such parent's rights with respect to the child.

Ethical

None of the religions—Judaism, Islam, Buddhism, and Christianity—approve of the abandonment of a child. The story of Moses being left so that the Pharaoh's daughter would be sure to find him is an example of the tender concern of a mother and father not to abandon their child. The disapproval of abandonment applies especially to an infant or a very young child.

In the United States today, the abandonment of parents by their runaway children is a reverse kind of abandonment. Both religious and secular agencies care for such runaways in numerous shelters and "safe places," some of which are sponsored by churches and synagogues.

Psychological

The parent who abandons a baby will likely suffer guilt, fear of being caught, remorse, shame, and other emotional difficulties.

54 ADOPTION

Legal

Adoption is a legal relationship in which a court establishes parent and child relations between two persons who are not biologically related to one another as parent and child.

Surprisingly to many, adoption as a legal institution is of quite recent origin; it did not exist historically in our law. Rather, persons, usually minors, who needed care were simply taken into the homes of relatives or neighbors and raised there along with the caretaker's own family. Thus did adoption exist in fact, if not in law. In this century adoption statutes were enacted in all states. Adoption provided a way for recreating parent-child relationships after existing relations were ended by death or termination of parental rights.

A child may not have more than one set of parents at the same time. Until the parental rights of the natural or birth parents are ended by death or termination, a child may not be adopted by others. If the natural or birth parents are alive, they must consent before their minor child can be adopted. Failure to obtain the knowing and voluntary consent of a parent would result in the invalidity of an adoption decree. Although most states provide that adoption decrees are final, cases are brought challenging a decree on the grounds that a parent did not freely consent or that a parent (typically the father) did not know of the proceeding and did not consent.

Early statutes varied concerning the rights of an adopted child, e.g. with respect to rights of inheritance from natural and adoptive parents and the relatives of such parents. Now most statutes provide that from the time of the final decree of adoption the adoptee is for all purposes the child of the adopters with exactly the same rights as their natural child and the parents have exactly the same parental duties as natural parents.

Most states also provide that an adult may be adopted, with the consent of the adoptee. The adults then have a parent-child relationship which will be effective for purposes of inheritance and other family provisions in the law.

Ethical

In Judaic and Christian scriptures there are only five references to adoption. (Romans 8:15, 23; 9:4; Galatians 4:5; Ephesians 1:5) In these, the term adoption is used as a metaphor to describe the way in which God adopts us in redemption, as God's children through redemption in Jesus Christ. Since the Apostle Paul used this as a metaphor in writing to the Romans and Ephesians, then the literal adoption of children by persons not their biological parents was a common experience in the Judaeo-Christian world. Furthermore, the process of adoption was a highly regarded way of parenting. Otherwise, this highly educated Jewish Christian would not have used the word adoption to describe the ultimate relationship of a person to God in Jesus Christ.

Islam does not permit adoption because a child cannot give proof of his or her parentage. Every child must be identified by and with his or her biological parents. If this is not possible, children are to be related to their "brothers in religion." Just how much such a practice is observed in a country where thousands of orphans are left by war is not possible to say. Nor is it clear to the Ethical Editor as to how Americanized Moslems will follow the American custom of adoption.

Buddhism's practices concerning adoption are not available to the Ethical Editor. American Buddhists may or may not follow American practices of adoption.

Finding adoptable children is difficult today because of the prevalence of abortion and the increasing number of single mothers who keep their babies instead of giving them up for adoption.

In Christianity, the Catholic Church, some Protestant churches, and some television ministries sponsor homes for unwed mothers; such homes often provide adoption services for the mother who chooses to adopt her child out. Christian churches have only positive approaches to adoption; they reach out and encompass the child into the church family as a "highly chosen child."

Psychological

A recent survey revealed that a group of teenage mothers who gave up their babies for adoption proved mostly to be more healthy mentally than similar teenagers who kept their babies; the former suffered fewer symptoms of emotional distress and experienced significantly higher levels of self-esteem.

An individual, a mother particularly but a father as well, can suffer guilt and remorse, from putting the baby up for adoption, but the Psychological Editor suspects the reaction may also be relief.

55 JUDGMENTS
Legal

A judgment for the support of a child is an order from a court that an individual found to be the parent or guardian of a child pay a specified amount for the support of the child.

Recent federal legislation requires that states formulate support schedules which determine the amount of support which is owed depending upon the income of the parents and the number of children.

In a dissolution action of marriage in which there are minor children, the court will provide for the custody of the children by giving the custody to one (sole custody) or both (joint custody) parents. One or both parents will be ordered to pay support. The court is not limited to the amount set forth in the support schedule but may determine support in accord with the needs of the child (including any special medical or emotional or educational needs), the ability of each parent to pay, any other financial resources the child may have, and the standard of living the child would have had if there had been no dissolution.

Child support judgments may also be entered in paternity actions in which a man is determined to be the father of the child and is ordered to pay support. The amount of support will depend upon the ability of the man to pay, the ability of the mother to contribute to the support of the child, and the child's needs.

Legislatures in recent years have become quite active in insisting upon the payment of child support. Statutes normally provide that any property of the parent may be levied upon for the collection of child support, the wages of the parent may be attached, and income tax refunds may be taken for child support. Failure to pay the full amount or to pay at all or to pay on time does not cancel the obligation; the parent to whom support is to be paid may bring a legal action for arrearage (the amount of past due child support) and may sue to collect amounts expended for child support which another was to provide even after the child reaches the age of majority.

If the state provides support, the parent who receives support assigns to the state the parent's right to collect support and the state will then become the party seeking support.

Psychological

The psychological state of a parent who ignores a child support judgment is highly variable.

Such parents are mostly fathers. Some are the working poor who labor hard to support two families, and are continually behind financially, but still suffer feelings of self-reproach, guilt, and inferiority. At the other extreme are the selfish who just don't care and try to avoid all responsibility.

ABORTION

Legalities

Webster's New World Dictionary, Third College Edition, (New York: Simon & Schuster, 1988) defines abortion as the expulsion of a human fetus within the early (first 12) weeks of pregnancy, before it is viable; and viable as "capable of living, growing, and developing."

Regarding an induced, elected abortion, the U.S. Supreme Court accepted, in *Roe v. Wade*, January 22, 1973, the constitutionality of the following definition of viability: "That stage of fetal development when the life of the unborn child may be continued indefinitely outside the womb by natural or artificial life-support systems." In accordance with this definition, the Supreme Court ruled that a state may choose to forbid abortions after the fetus is viable; before viability, the female may choose to terminate the pregnancy, although after the first trimester the state may make regulations reasonably relating to the female's health.

This decision established the principle that constitutional protection of the life of the fetus applied only to a viable fetus; that is, before viability, a fetus would not be regarded legally as a person entitled to constitutional protections. As a result of *Roe*, state abortion laws making all abortions criminal were struck down as unconstitutional.

However, as of July 3, 1989, by a 5-4 decision in *Webster v. Reproductive Health Services*, the Supreme Court upheld a Missouri law which:

Prohibits an induced abortion in a public hospital (unless the mother's life is at risk);

179

Forbids the spending of state money for counseling a female about induced abortions; and

Requires a test by a physician after 20 weeks of gestation, if such a test will help to determine the potential viability of the fetus outside the womb.

This decision continues to recognize that the time of viability may be difficult to determine and may vary among pregnancies. The state may require a medical practitioner who reasonably suspects that the fetus may be viable to conduct further tests to determine more accurately if the fetus is viable.

Further, as of June 25, 1990, by a 5-4 decision, in *Hodgson v. Minnesota,* and by a 6-3 decision in *Ohio v. Akron Center for Reproductive Health,* the Supreme Court upheld two more state laws. These laws prohibit a minor from having an induced abortion without first obtaining permission of:

Both parents, or, without notifying her parents, the permission of a judge who determines that she is mature enough to give consent to an abortion, or if she is not sufficiently mature, that an abortion would be in her best interests (Minnesota);

One parent, or the right to obtain in a court procedure a determination like the one above from a judge (Ohio).

The Court's action in the two above cases may, by implication, have validated parental-involvement laws in other states including Arkansas, Georgia, Illinois, Kentucky, Nebraska, Nevada, Utah, and West Virginia.

The Supreme Court has also agreed to review other restrictive state laws, one of which regulates out-patient abortion clinics.

Thus, the constitutional right established in *Roe* of a female (see 56 PATERNAL RIGHTS) to have an induced abortion before the fetus becomes viable has not been denied, but the power of the various states to restrict and regulate that right has been reaffirmed.

Politics

Abortion remains a highly charged emotional issue with the U.S. public. On the one hand, the "right to life" or "pro-life" persons maintain the view that viability is not the proper test, that life begins with conception, and that abortion is murder. On the other hand, the "freedom of choice" or "pro-choice" persons assert that a female's body is subject to control only by her own conscience and that her "right to choose" cannot be taken from her by the dictates of others.

Following the *Webster* decision, the abortion issue remains a complex and difficult social and political issue. The various parties will continue their struggle not only in the Supreme Court, but also in state legislatures. Pending the Supreme Court's likely re-examination of the issue, restrictive and non-restrictive measures will be supported and contested in state legislatures.

Besides the polarized views that abortion should be completely unregulated, or that abortion is murder under any circumstances, there are a variety of intermediate positions. One is that abortion is justified, but only in early stages and if the pregnancy results from rape or incest, if it threatens the life of the pregnant female, or if prenatal tests establish that the fetus would develop into a hopelessly and tragically deformed and handicapped baby. See 48 FETAL MONITORING.

Asserting that every elective abortion is a tragedy, the former Surgeon General of the United States (C. Everett Koop, MD, who has acknowledged a strong pro-life bias) said: "If you want to get rid of abortions, you better get rid of the reason for them—unwanted pregnancies."

The teaching and acceptance of abstinence, or of birth control by at least one method, might prove to be the one course politically acceptable to both pro-choice and pro-life extremes.

Types

Medically there are two general types of abortion:

Spontaneous abortions, which are known commonly and medically as miscarriages (see FULL TERM PREGNANCY, pages 157, 158.); and

Induced or elective abortions, which involve deliberate, voluntary terminations of pregnancy.

Several procedures are available to induce abortions; choice of procedure depends to a degree on the stage of the pregnancy.

Menstrual extraction is sometimes used within two weeks following a missed menstrual period. The entire uterine lining, including any embryo, is extracted by vacuum through an inserted tube. See 57 MENSTRUAL EXTRACTION.

Vacuum suction curettage is usually used between the seventh and twelfth weeks of pregnancy (but may be used as late as the fifteenth week). The fetus (which can be seen at this point) is removed by suction through a tube; thereafter the uterine lining is scraped with a spoonlike curet to remove placental tissue not vacuumed out. See 58 VACUUM SUCTION CURETTAGE.

Uterine contraction is usually used after the fifteenth week of pregnancy (but possibly as early as the twelfth week). The uterus is made to contract, much as in natural labor, in reaction to the introduction of a saline solution or the hormone prostaglandin; the contraction evacuates the fetus. See 59 UTERINE CONTRACTION.

Hysterotomy is a late pregnancy procedure. The abdomen and uterus are surgically cut, and the fetus is removed; this procedure is much like a delivery by Cesarean section. See 60 HYSTEROTOMY.

Only a qualified physician in a medical office, clinic, or hospital should perform these procedures.

There are, however, efforts being made to enable females to perform abortions without the assistance of medical personnel. A kit, selling for under $100, for use by a female with help from another person, is said to use the menstrual extraction technique and be for use through the eighth week of pregnancy, although some medical authorities say that menstrual extraction should be performed in the first two weeks after a missed period. The use of such kits and their manufacture and sale in some jurisdictions may be criminal offenses. See 57 MENSTRUAL EXTRACTION; see also 61 SELF ABORTION.

In France, a German drug, sometimes called the morning after pill, is used by females to slough off the uterine lining and embryo, in the early stages of pregnancy in a privately induced abortion. See RU 486, Glossary. The French health minister, recognizing the state's inability to regulate what persons do with respect to abortion privately, has stated: "Morally this product belongs to women." The drug is under study in the U.S. and may eventually be approved by the Food and Drug Administration (FDA) for sale in the U.S. See 61 SELF ABORTION.

Induced abortions are elected for a variety of reasons, such as: to protect the life of the pregnant female in a therapeutic abortion; to prevent the fathering of a child by rape or incest; to avoid giving birth to a hopelessly abnormal baby; or, controversially, simply to avoid motherhood.

Risks

The former Surgeon General has also reported that induced "...abortion imposes a relatively low psychological risk..." for females; but that "...there is no doubt that some people have severe psychological effects after abortion." See 62 ABORTIONS. However, a panel of the American Psychological Association, as reported by *Time* (March 27, 1989, p. 82) concluded, after study, that induced "...abortion inflicts no particular damage on women..." generally; and that "...there has been no rise in mental illness..." accompanying the millions of abortions following the 1973 legalization.

The medical risk of abortion varies with the individual female, her age and health, weeks of gestation, the technique used, who performs the abortion, and where it is done. See 63 INCAPACITATION.

Clinics

Before the 1973 legalization of abortion in the U.S., many illegal induced abortions, sometimes called coathanger abortions, were performed in unsanitary conditions by unqualified persons, often with tragic physical and emotional consequences (see 64 ILLEGAL) for the pregnant female. Now, in almost all major cities, abortions are performed (see 65 COSTS) legally in hygienic hospitals and clinics by qualified physicians. The location of such establishments can be ascertained from obstetricians, gynecologists, and family physicians, or, in some metropolitan areas, from the telephone book *Yellow Pages*.

Counsel

Some pregnant females wish to seek counsel before deciding whether or not to have an abortion. Abortion counseling services are also advertised in the *Yellow Pages*. Such services are likely to be strong proponents of either the pro-life or the pro-choice view. A decision after consideration of both views will perhaps give the greatest personal satisfaction. One's personal physician may be of great help.

Incidence

Since 1973, the number of legally induced abortions in the U.S. as reported by the U.S. Department of Health and Human Services has increased from 763,500 in 1974 to 1,353,700 in 1987. In 1987 such abortions were distributed approximately as follows:

			%
Years of age	Under 20	349,300	25.8
	20-24	452,100	33.4
	25 and over	552,300	40.8
	Total	1,353,700	100.0
Marital Status	Married	368,200	27.2
	Unmarried	985,500	72.8
	Total	1,353,700	100.0
Weeks of Gestation	Under 8 weeks	682,300	50.4
	9-10	352,000	26.0
	11-12	167,800	12.4
	13-15	83,900	6.2
	16-20	56,900	4.2
	21 and over	10,800	0.8
	Total	1,353,700	100.0

In all states the legal age for marriage without the parents' consent is 18, except in Rhode Island, where it is 21. How many of the 349,300 abortions under the age of 20 were under the legal age for marriage without the parents' consent is not known; but a substantial number seems probable.

---

56 PATERNAL RIGHTS

Legal

If the father is married to the mother at the time of conception or birth of the child, the father and mother share identical parental rights. If the parents' marriage is dissolved, the court will determine parental rights in awarding sole custody to one parent (which may be the mother or the father, they are to receive equal consideration for custody) or legal custody to both parents (joint custody) and physical custody to mother or father. See 51 CUSTODY.

If the mother is not married or is not married to the father at the time when the child is conceived or born, then the mother has all parental rights. The father has parental rights only from the time he is recognized by the court as a father. See 49 PATERNITY. A man does not have parental rights simply because his name appears on the birth certificate as father, because he is recognized by mother and child as father, or because he voluntarily supports the child.

Once the unmarried father is legally recognized and has paternal rights, the situation becomes much like that of parents whose marriage is dissolved. If the court awards joint custody, the father has the right to participate in and make decisions about the child's education, health care and religion. If the mother is awarded sole custody, she alone may make all decisions concerning the child.

A statute or court decision may determine whose name the child born out of wedlock will carry.

Paternal rights include the right to the companionship of the child and once recognized as father a man will have a right to visitation unless the mother can prove that visitation with the father will seriously harm or endanger the child.

Whether he is married to the mother or not, the father after the time of conception has no right to make or be involved in the decision concerning the termination of the pregnancy. See 62 ABORTIONS. The mother is not legally obligated to seek the father's advice or permission about an abortion. In fact, there is no legal obligation upon the mother to even inform a man that she is pregnant and believes he is the father.

57   MENSTRUAL EXTRACTION
Medical

This procedure is sometimes used in the first two weeks after a missed menstrual period before pregnancy is confirmed. It may be performed by a physician, in his or her office; a local anesthetic may or may not be used. As a means of avoiding pregnancy, a high percentage of failures occurs; fortunately menstrual extraction is not widely practiced.

Self-administered menstrual extraction may be safer than an amateur coat-hanger abortion, or an amateur abortion induced by uterine infusion of an acidic solution such as a carbonated beverage, but only if done by a person who understands the procedure. Often the procedure results in severe pelvic infection, especially if practiced by an unqualified person in unsanitary conditions.

Legal

The use of menstrual extraction self-help kits to induce an abortion may be punished as a criminal act. See 61 SELF ABORTION. The manufacture, sale and distribution of these kits or of information about how to make and use them may likewise be criminalized under abortion laws and laws prohibiting the unlicensed practice of medicine.

A defendant who is charged with a criminal offense for providing the means to perform self abortions or who is ordered to cease providing these means may claim that his First Amendment rights (freedom of speech) have been violated. It is unclear at the moment whether this defense is viable.

58   VACUUM SUCTION CURETTAGE
Medical

This procedure is normally used from the seventh though the twelfth week of pregnancy (sometimes as late at the fifteenth week), after pregnancy is established. The procedure is performed in a clinic or a hospital's outpatient department; it may involve either a local or a general anesthetic. Most females recover from vacuum suction curettage quickly; sexual intercourse is usually possible several weeks after the treatment.

59   UTERINE CONTRACTION
Medical

This procedure, which is normally used with analgesics after the fifteenth week (sometimes as early as the twelfth week), requires hospitalization for one to two days. Uterine contraction is induced by injecting a saline solution or prostaglandin through the abdomen into the amniotic fluid, or by infusing either substance through the vagina and cervix to lodge between the placenta and uterine wall. This induced contraction expels the fetus usually in about 12 hours. Recovery takes longer than from vacuum suction curettage.

60   HYSTEROTOMY

Medical

This procedure is a late pregnancy one requiring hospitalization; it is the most complicated and risky abortion procedure, and is not much practiced now. The female's abdomen and uterus are opened surgically, and the fetus and placenta are removed. See Cesarean section, Glossary.

61   SELF ABORTION

Medical

Self-abortion by RU 486 (mifepristone) is currently being tested experimentally in this country; side effects have not been wholly determined. Asserting that RU 486 may be safer and cheaper than surgical abortion, and in addition may be useful in treating certain diseases, a panel of the American Medical Association, backed by the AMA House of Delegates, strongly supports such testing. (*The Courier Journal* [Louisville], June 28, 1990)

Legal

Self abortion is a crime in some states. This is so even if the abortion is performed on a previable fetus; however, self abortion of a viable fetus is the more serious offense.

Under the guidelines set forth by the United States Supreme Court in *Roe v. Wade*, the state is able to impose reasonable regulations governing abortions as medical procedures. A permissible regulation is the requirement that a licensed physician perform an otherwise legal abortion.

62   ABORTIONS

Legal

In 1973 in the *Roe v. Wade* decision the United States Supreme Court held that a pregnant woman's decision whether to terminate a pregnancy was included within a zone of privacy entitled to protection under the Constitution. Other protected decisions include those concerning use of contraceptives and parental decisions about child rearing and education. The *Roe* decision meant that state laws making abortion a crime could not be enforced. Since 1973 clinics in which abortions are performed and ads for abortion services and counseling have become common, especially in larger cities.

The decision of the Supreme Court recognized three separate stages in pregnancy and balanced the interests of the pregnant woman, the public, and the developing fetus at different stages. In the first trimester (approximately the first three months of pregnancy, 12-14 weeks) the woman and her physician may decide whether to continue the pregnancy. State regulation at this period will be minimal if the woman is not a minor (18 or older).

From the end of the first trimester, the government may make regulations which are related to the pregnant woman's health. These will include such things as licensed clinics, licensed health professionals, and support services related to maternal health. From the time when the fetus is viable [that is, able to live outside the womb with or without life support assistance (respirators, etc.)], the state may choose to forbid abortions altogether. The state may also require tests to determine whether the fetus is viable.

If the pregnant woman is a minor (not yet 18 years old and unmarried), she must either have the permission of her parent or parents for an abortion (as for any other medical procedure upon minors) or seek a judicial bypass. A judicial bypass is a determination by a court that it would not be in the best interests of the minor to seek parental consent for an abortion and either a finding that the minor is mature enough to make the decision about abortion for herself or the court will make whatever decision it determines is in her best interests.

There is no legally enforceable role for the father (whether married to the mother or not) in her abortion decision.

Ethical

Orthodox Judaism "legalizes" abortion to save the life of the mother. Among more liberal Orthodox Jews this principle is expanded to include the mental health of the mother, being aware of the possibility of depression and the threat of suicide in some pregnant women. Reform and Conservative Judaism permit abortion for unselfish reasons.

Islam is divided on the issue of abortion. Some Muslim thinkers oppose abortion on the basis of Koran verses which say "Do not kill your children for fear of heresy. He will provide for both you and them. Your needs depend on Allah and he will provide them. He who avoids Allah's wrath, Allah will find a way out for him, and will provide for him in a way he had not expected."

Other Muslim thinkers believe that Islam does not forbid abortion within the first 120 days of pregnancy. They argue that such a position makes things easier for people, by preventing feelings of shame. Especially is this so if a woman has had excessive pregnancies and fears another; or if she suffers weakness as a result of repeated pregnancies.

Some Buddhists might interpret the first of the Five Precepts: To abstain from taking life, as a prohibition. The Ethical Editor is not aware of a specific set of Buddhist teachings on abortion and asks the help of any reader who might know of such. American Buddhists are probably divided in their beliefs about abortion, as are Muslims and Christians.

The Catholic encyclical of 1966, *Humanae Vitae*, condemns any directly willed or procured abortion, even for therapeutic purposes. The only allowable abortion "...is when the killing of the fetus is indirect and performed to save the life of the mother, such as in the case of a cancerous uterus or an ectopic pregnancy." Many groups of Protestants and non-Catholics such as Mormons, and many fundamentalist churches, have beliefs about abortion similar to Catholic belief. Moderate and liberal Catholics and Protestants teach that instances such as rape, incest, the mental health of the mother and the pregnancy of exceptionally young mothers justify abortion.

Large numbers of Jews and Christians believe firmly in freedom of the woman to choose abortion; and in her power of decision relative to her own body.

Psychological

Before and after an abortion, especially a first abortion, a pregnant female usually experiences ambivalence about whether she's doing the right thing, and fear, apprehension, and anxiety possibly heightened by guilt. Such distress is usually greater before the abortion.

After the abortion, most feel a sense of relief but with the usual multifactorial individual variations. Severe negative reactions are relatively infrequent.

A recent survey revealed that young females who had abortions were, when older, more mentally healthy than those who kept their babies, or than those who gave their babies up for adoption.

63 INCAPACITATION

Medical

If a legal abortion is expertly performed, there is little likelihood of medical damage to the female. If illegally and inexpertly performed, the female may be damaged by instrumentation and hemorrhage; and by infection leading to severe illness, hysterectomy, and possibly death.

64 ILLEGAL

Psychological

Where abortion is illegal, society may be especially punitive and pejorative toward a female who has an abortion which, if discovered, increases her stress. Even if undiscovered, she may suffer guilt for deception and for having committed an illegal act.

65 COSTS

Medical

Legal abortions cost approximately $175 to $225; or in some clinics, for free if the patient is unable to pay; such abortions are done very quickly on out patients by people with great expertise. Illegal abortions can be arranged, but any cost may be assessed.

ADDENDUM

ABOUT THE GLOSSARY

There are a number of words and phrases which have not yet found their ways into Random House and Webster dictionaries, but which will do so in future editions because of growing general usage.

Having no guidance from the dictionaries, the Editors have interpreted what persons have in mind when they use such words and phrases.

The phrase "having sex" is an example. The phrase is not recognized yet by Random House or Webster but it is in daily—or even hourly—use by the oral and written media. What kind of sex is meant by the phrase "having sex": sexual intercourse only; or homosexuality; or any kind of sexual engagement; or sometimes one kind of activity and sometimes another? Recent trends in today's society, at least in the media, have been "toward anything goes," and for this reason the Editors have defined "having sex" as "Participating in any form of sexual activity, free from injury, pain, or physical damage." The Editors realize that all persons may not accept this definition.

The phrase "oral sex" is not in the dictionaries, either, but is in general use. The Editors have decided that the users probably mean (rather than fellatio or cunnilingus) "...any form of sexual stimulation by means of the mouth or tongue, but without injury or pain."

Another example: "sexual preference." This is a phrase made popular by homosexuals and their supporters, who are striving for social and legal acceptance, and who may have in mind a preference between sexual intercourse and homosexuality. The Editors have settled on this definition:

195

"A phrase ... implying acceptance without opprobrium of many forms of a person's sexual behavior, without the infliction of injury or damage."

With respect to *some* words in the sexual vocabulary, Webster and Random House have already recognized a trend toward anything goes. See these examples:

Webster's *New International Dictionary* (Springfield: Merriam) 1933	*Webster's* *New World Dictionary* Third College Edition (New York: Simon & Schuster) 1988
Homosexuality	
Med. Morbid sexual passion for one of the same sex.	Of or characterized by sexual desire for those of the same sex as oneself.
Masturbation	
Onanism; self-pollution.	The manipulation of one's own genitals, or the genitals of (another), for sexual gratification.
Gay	
adj. Merry.	adj. Joyous and lively; merry; happy; lighthearted. n. A homosexual; esp. a homosexual man.

So far as the Editors can determine, the 1933 definition of homosexuality really did reflect the opinion of the medical profession at the time. The modern medical view of the majority is that homosexuality is an alternative life-style in which the sexual object happens to be a person of the same sex.

Note the major change in the meaning of "masturbation" brought about by usage and recorded by Webster, in only a half a century: "self-pollution" in 1933 but "gratification" in 1988. Note also "gay" is still "merry" as an adjective; but now it has become a noun as well.

The Editors have accepted the view that sexual intercourse is "genital contact, esp. the insertion of the penis into the vagina followed by ejaculation; coitus; copulation." (*The Random House College Dictionary*, Revised Edition, [New York: Random House, 1988]) Opinion is now divided as to whether or not homosexuality and anal sex are "natural." The Editors have decided to remain neutral on the subject even though the law in many jurisdictions still refers to some or all of such activities as "against nature" and, except as between husband and wife, illegal.

The Editors.

Abbreviations

adj.	adjective
e.g.	for example
esp.	especially
i.e.	that is
n.	noun
pl.	plural
sing.	singular
v.	verb

GLOSSARY

abdomen n. The cavity in the body containing digestive organs such as the stomach, intestines, and liver. adj. **abdominal.**

abortion n. The early expulsion of a fetus before it can survive outside of the uterus or womb, esp. an expulsion induced or elected. See **elective abortion, induced abortion, miscarriage, therapeutic abortion.**

abscess n. Pus accumulated from broken-down tissue; usually tender and painful.

abstinence n. Self-denial; doing without voluntarily. adj. **abstinent.** See **celibacy, chastity.**

abuse n. Improper usage; maltreatment emotionally, orally, mentally or physically. See **child abuse, substance abuse.**

accusation n. A formal charge of an alleged, legally punishable offense.

acquired immune deficiency syndrome See **AIDS.**

acquired immunity An immunity acquired during life; e.g. naturally after an infectious disease such as chicken pox; or artificially as by vaccination.

actionable adj. Affording legal ground for a suit to be tried in court.

acute adj. Highly sensitive; sudden, sharp as an acute pain. See **chronic.**

acyclovir n. A synthetic antiviral drug, particularly used in the treatment of herpes simplex virus infections.

ad litem For the defense or prosecution of a suit. See **guardian ad litem.**

addict n. A compulsive, obsessive user of a substance such as, for example, a drug such as heroin.

adolescent n. A teenager; a boy or girl beyond puberty but before adulthood, usually experiencing marked physical, psychological, and emotional change as part of the maturation process.

adoption n. The court ordered transfer of a child's legal rights and duties from natural to adoptive parents.

adult n. A fully developed organism; also, a person who has attained the age of legal competence which, in almost all states, is 18 years of age.

adultery n. Voluntary sexual intercourse between a husband or a wife and a person other than the spouse. See **fornication.**

AFDC Aid to Families with Dependent Children. A governmental program, usually federally and state funded and state operated, that provides financial assistance to families with small children and with incomes below a certain level.

199

affinity n. A close relationship; a relationship of persons by marriage rather than by blood. See **consanguinity**.

afterbirth See **placenta**.

age of consent The age at which a person can legally consent, for example, to marriage without parental approval; or to lawful sexual intercourse. See **abortion, child abuse, consent, statutory rape**.

Aid to Families with Dependent Children See **AFDC**.

AIDS (acquired immune deficiency syndrome) A pathologic condition, eventually fatal, in which the immune system fails to provide normal protection from infections.

AIDS-related complex See **ARC**.

alienation of affection A third party's malicious and willful interference with a marriage relationship without just excuse; it may be legally actionable in some places.

allergy n. Hypersensitivity to a substance or a condition. adj. **allergic**.

amino acid One of a large group of organic compounds which are necessary for growth and function of the body. Proteins are made from a smaller group of 20 amino acids, assembled in a wide variety of configurations.

amniocentesis n. The surgical removal by hollow needle of amniotic fluid in order to determine various fetal characteristics.

amnion n. The sac within the uterus which surrounds the fetus during pregnancy. adj. **amnionic, amniotic**.

amniotic fluid The watery fluid which is in the amnion and surrounds the fetus during pregnancy. It cradles the fetus and facilitates the exchange of matter between mother and fetus.

amphotericin B n. A drug effective in the treatment of certain fungal infections.

analgesic n. A substance that relieves pain; e.g. aspirin.

anemia n. A deficiency in the hemoglobin content of the blood, or of red blood corpuscles, often caused by insufficient iron in the diet. Weakness, fatigue, breathlessness, and headache are symptoms.

anesthesia n. A general or local loss of feeling, esp. pain, induced by disease or drugs.

anesthetic n. A pain-relieving drug. adj. **anesthetic**.

aneurysm n. A permanent or extending dilatation of a blood vessel wall which has been weakened by a disease such as syphilis.

annulment n. The voiding by competent authority; the assertion that a marital status never existed. See **divorce, dissolution of marriage**.

antepartum hemorrhage A uterine hemorrhage occurring before childbirth.

anti- A prefix meaning against, opposed to.

antibiotic n. A drug such as penicillin or streptomycin capable of slowing the growth of, or destroying, certain bacteria; often used to treat infectious diseases. See **broad spectrum antibiotic**.

antibody n. A protein produced by lymphocytes which neutralizes an antigen to help the body destroy invading microorganisms.

antidepressant n. Any drug used to treat mental or emotional depression.

antifungal n. An agent destructive of fungi or preventive of the growth of fungi; e.g. griseofulvin or amphotericin B.

antigen n. A substance that stimulates the production of antibodies in the body's defense against infection and disease.

antiviral n. A drug destructive of viruses. adj. **antiviral.**

anus n. The opening in the rectum through which feces are excreted. adj. **anal.**

anxiety n. An abnormal, tense feeling, often without cause, of being powerless to cope with events; concern or apprehension about the future; tension with sweating and trembling sometimes accompanies the feeling.

aorta n. The main artery of the blood circulatory system delivering blood from the heart to the entire body, except to the lungs.

aortic heart valve The valve between the aorta and the heart which prevents blood from flowing backwards into the heart.

appendicitis n. Inflammation of the appendix.

appendix n. A vermiform (wormlike) tube with no known function, attached to the large intestine.

ARC (AIDS-related complex) A combination of disorders and symptoms that is often a prelude to AIDS.

artery n. Any blood vessel functioning to convey blood away from the heart. adj. **arterial.**

arthritis n. Inflammation of a joint or joints. adj. **arthritic.**

artificial insemination The injection of sperm into the vagina by an instrument rather than by coitus.

aspiration n. The withdrawal by suction of fluids or tissue; also, the act of inhaling.

aspirin n. Acetylsalicylic acid; a drug used to reduce fever and relieve pain; an analgesic.

assault n. An attack, actual or threatened; rape. See **battery, rape, sexual assault.**

asymptomatic adj. Free from symptoms or from personally perceived complaints.

atom n. The smallest part of an element that can chemically react.

attachment n. The process of bringing person or property into the custody of the court, esp. to prevent the dissipation before trial of a defendant's property.

azidothymidine See **zidovudine.**

AZT (azidothymidine) See **zidovudine.**

bacterial culture See **culture.**

bacterium n. Any of various microscopic organisms occurring in air, water, and soil, some of which cause disease and which are usually classified by their shapes: rod (bacillus); spherical (coccus); comma (vibrio); spiral (spirochete) pl. **bacteria,** adj. **bacterial.**

bad blood Slang for syphilis.

balm n. An aromatic, healing ointment.

Bartholin's gland One of two small glands on either side of the vaginal opening, which secrete mucus; the glands are easily infected and may become painfully swollen and abscessed.

basal adj. Basic; fundamental.

bastard n. The legal reference to a child born outside of marriage; however, the term would not now be an appropriate legal manner of referring to such a person, having become through common use an insult.

battery n. The use of force to injure another person esp. following a threat of violence which is sometimes referred to as assault, hence the phrase "assault and battery." See **assault**.

benign adj. Gentle; kind; not malignant.

bile n. A greenish yellow liquid secreted by the liver that is stored in the gallbladder and passed into the digestive tract to aid digestion and absorb fats; also called gall.

biopsy n. Diagnostic examination, often by microscope, of tissues or fluids removed from the body.

birth control See **contraception**.

birth mother The female who carries a fetus to term and through whose birth canal the baby is delivered.

bisexual adj. Sexually attracted to both males and females.

bladder n. A sac (pouch) that stores a gas or liquid; esp. urinary bladder which stores urine.

bleeder n. A hemophiliac; that is, one with an undue tendency to bleed.

blindness n. Lacking the ability to see; sightlessness.

blister n. A swelling on the skin or mucous surface filled with fluid or serum.

blood n. The fluid that is pumped through the body by the heart.

blood count The number of red and white blood cells, and platelets, in a given quantity of blood.

blood pressure The force per unit of area, against the walls of the arteries, of the blood pumped by the heart.

blood serum See **serum**.

blood sugar Glucose; a normal and essential sugar in the blood.

blood test A test to analyze the structure and makeup of the blood, commonly a test for syphilis.

blood vessel A tube through which the blood circulates in the body.

boil n. A pus-filled, locally infected, inflammation of the skin.

Borrelia burgdorferi A bacterium causing Lyme disease, transmitted by a certain tick.

bowel n. All or part of the intestines.

brain n. The organ of thought located in the skull, which controls the mental and physical actions of the body.

brain death The state of the body in which consciousness has been permanently lost but the heart continues to beat. See **death**.

breach of duty Failure to perform a legal or moral duty, esp. an official or fiduciary duty.

breast n. One of two glands surrounding a nipple and protruding from the chest, far more developed in the female than in the male. Female breasts are the source of human milk for newborns.

breast examination The examination of the breast to detect changes, such as lumps, which may indicate the onset of disease. Self-examination monthly is recommended by some physicians for females.

broad spectrum antibiotic An antibiotic effective against many kinds of bacteria.

brothel n. A house for prostitutes; a bawdy house; a house of ill repute.

bubo n. An enlarged and inflamed lymph gland, esp. in the armpit or groin, often tender and painful.

buggery n. Sodomy. See **sodomy**.

buttock n. Either of two masses of muscle and tissue constituting the seat of the body. Usually **buttocks**.

Caesarean section See **Cesarean section**.

calcium n. A chemical element essential and abundant in the bones, teeth, fluids and tissues of the body.

calory (calorie) n. The amount of heat required to increase the temperature of a gram of water one degree Celsius. adj. **caloric**.

cancer n. A malignant growth of cells which often spreads to interfere, often fatally, with normal functions of the body.

Candida albicans n. The fungus that causes candidiasis, a common yeast infection.

candidiasis n. A fungal infection often affecting the skin, mouth, or vagina.

cardiac n. A person suffering from a disorder of the heart. adj. Pertaining to the heart.

caries n. Decay of a bone or tooth; esp. tooth decay.

carrier n. One who harbors an infectious disease that can be transmitted to others, but who may enjoy some immunity and freedom from symptoms.

cathartic n. A substance that induces evacuation of the bowel; a laxative.

caustic n. An agent that uses chemical action to burn or destroy tissue.

cauterization n. Tissue destruction by burning or searing with an electric spark, a heated instrument, or by application of a caustic. v. **cauterize**

cavity n. A hollow space in a mass such as the body, a bone, an organ, or a tooth.

ceftriaxone n. A broad spectrum antibiotic used in treatment of gonorrhea. See **Rocephin**.

celibacy n. State of being unmarried; also, abstinence from sexual intercourse. See **chaste**.

cell n. A living unitary structure, usually microscopic; the fundamental structural unit of a living organism.

centigrade adj. A scale for measuring temperature that fixes the freezing point of water at zero degrees, and the boiling point of water at 100 degrees above zero; abbreviated C (compare Fahrenheit).

cervical cancer A malignant tumor of the neck of the uterus (cervix).

cervicitis n. Fungal, bacterial, viral, or other infection of the cervix.

cervix n. The neck of an organ; esp. the constricted end or neck of the uterus.

Cesarean section Delivery of a baby surgically by incision of the abdomen and uterus. (Julius Caesar is supposed to have been delivered by such section; hence, the name.)

chancre n. A sore or ulcer usually with a hard rim or base; esp. the initial (primary) sore of syphilis.

chancroid n. A painful genital ulcer, sexually transmitted; a soft chancre.

chaste adj. Innocent of sexual intercourse; sexually abstinent; decent; undefiled. See **abstinence, celibacy, chastity.**

chastity n. The condition of being chaste; virginity; decency. See **virgin.**

child abuse Neglect, exploitation, or physical, mental, emotional, sexual or moral harm of a minor. See **age of consent, consent, statutory rape.**

Chlamydia trachomatis The species of the bacteria chlamydiae that infects humans.

chlamydia n. A microscopic organism, recently classified as a bacterium, that is a common cause of urethritis, cervicitis, and serious eye infections. pl. **chlamydiae**, adj. **chlamydial.**

chlorophyll n. A green pigment, found in certain plants, that enables photosynthesis.

chromosome n. A structure within a cell nucleus which contains and transmits DNA.

chronic adj. Of long duration or of frequent recurrence.

cicatrix n. A scar.

civil incest See **incest.**

civil law Law, in contrast to criminal law, pertaining to the individual's private rights. See **criminal law.**

clap n. Slang for gonorrhea; usually referred to as "the clap."

clinic n. A facility equipped to provide medical services to patients, and/or to teach medical students. adj. **clinical.**

clitoris n. A small, erogenous, and erectile structure situated within the labia minora and above the urethral opening in the female.

clotrimazole n. An antifungal agent effective against many kinds of fungi.

cohabit v. To live together as husband and wife or as if husband and wife.

coitus n. Sexual intercourse. See **copulation, sexual intercourse.**

colon n. Part of the large intestine leading from the small intestine to the rectum.

colpitis n. Vaginitis.

colposcope, colpomicroscope n. An instrument using illumination and magnification that enables the visual examination of the upper vagina. adj. **colposcopic.**

common law marriage A valid legal marriage which is entered, if so provided by state law, without the usual formalities and solemnization (e.g. license, exchange of promises, witnesses, officiant) and is recognized on the basis of the parties' agreement to marry, living together as husband and wife, and public recognition as a married couple.

common law Unwritten secular law based on traditional English and American customs and court decisions, rather than legislated law.

compound n. A substance resulting from the chemical union of two or more elements in fixed proportions, such as water (H_2O) or salt (NaCl).

conception n. Fertilization of an ovum by a sperm cell; the inception or beginning of pregnancy.

condom n. A tubular sheath fitted over the penis to reduce the chance of venereal infection, or of conception, during sexual intercourse; slang terms: rubber, safe, skin.

congenital adj. Existing at birth. See **familial, hereditary.**

consanguinity n. Kinship by blood relationship of persons descended from a common ancestor. See **affinity.**

consent n. Voluntary agreement; generally, consent can only be given by one who has sufficient knowledge of the situation and freedom of choice; consent may be weakened or taken away altogether by force, fear, drugs, alcohol, lack of age and maturity, threats, intimidation, or ignorance. See **age of consent, statutory rape.**

constipation n. A condition of the bowels making the elimination of feces difficult or infrequent.

constitutional law The constitution of a state and law interpreted in relation thereto.

consummation n. Generally, a completion, fulfillment; specifically, to make a marriage complete by sexual intercourse. v. **consummate**

contagious adj. Capable of disease transmission by direct or indirect contact.

contraception n. The intentional avoidance of conception by preventing fertilization of the ovum; birth control.

contract v. To acquire an infection or disease; an agreement enforceable in law between tow or more competent parties to perform or not to perform specified acts.

contraindicate v. To render inadvisable, esp. the usual treatment or drug; e.g. an indicated treatment by penicillin of a person allergic to penicillin, is contraindicated. n. **contraindication.**

controlled substance A substance, esp. a drug, classified and controlled by law with respect to its sale and use.

convulsion n. A violent muscle spasm.

cooties n. Slang for an infestation of crab lice.

copulation n. Male and female sexual union; coitus. v. **copulate.** See **coitus, sexual intercourse.**

corpuscle n. A blood cell. See **hemoglobin.**

crab See **crab louse.**

crab louse n. Small sucking insect (Pediculus pubis), parasitic on man, transmitted by direct or genital contact to infest the skin and particularly its hairs. pl. **crab lice.**

crabs n. Slang for an infestation of crab lice.

criminal conversation Sexual intercourse with a husband or a wife by an outsider; defilement of a marriage; breach of the marriage covenant. Possibly still legally actionable in some states.

criminal law Law which, to protect society, defines harmful conduct and punishments therefor; such laws are generally described in criminal or penal codes. See **civil law.**

criminal prosecution Prosecution by the state in the interest of the public to convict one accused of crime.

cruelty n. The willful and unwarranted infliction of pain, emotional, mental or physical, on a living creature.

cryosurgery n. Surgery performed by freezing, for example with liquid nitrogen.

culture n. The growing of microorganisms such as bacteria for scientific study or medicinal use; a laboratory test to identify and grow organisms connected with an inflammation.

cunnilingus n. Stimulation of the female genitalia orally.

curet n. A spoonlike surgical instrument used for tissue removal by scraping.

curettage n. Surgical scraping for removal of tissue.

cystitis n. Inflammation of the inner lining of a sac or bladder, caused by an infection, frequently of the urinary bladder.

cytoplasm n. The substance surrounding the nucleus of a cell.

damages n. Money claimed by or awarded to a person injured by another, to compensate for loss resulting from the injury. See **punitive damages.**

DDI (dideoxyinosine) A drug that is chemically related to AZT, both of which are used in the treatment of AIDS.

death n. The state of the body in which all vital functions have irreversibly stopped. See **brain death.**

decree n. The declaration of an order of a court.

defecation n. The discharge of feces through the anus from the lower bowel.

defendant n. The person defending against a civil suit or criminal accusation. See **plaintiff.**

dementia n. Progressive mental deterioration, esp. of memory, judgment, and orientation, which occurs in third stage syphilis.

deoxyribonucleic acid See **DNA.**

depression n. A neurotic emotional condition, usually involving feelings of hopelessness, inadequacy, and the like.

desiccate v. To dry thoroughly. n. **desiccation.**

detoxify v. To remove or neutralize the effect of poison. n. **detoxification.**

deviation n. Variance from an established or customary norm; a change in original terms.

diabetes mellitus A disorder of the body's metabolism characterized by an excess of sugar in the blood and sometimes a deficiency of insulin. See **insulin**.

diaphragm n. The partition of muscle that separates the cavities of the chest and the abdomen; a contraceptive dome, made of rubber or plastic, to fit over the cervix of the uterus.

diarrhea n. Loose, watery stools in excessively frequent bowel movements.

dideoxyinosine See **DDI**.

dilation n. The natural or induced widening or enlargement of a body opening such as the cervix, in giving birth.

disease n. An abnormal condition or function of the body caused by infection, diet, heredity, toxins, tumors, or other injurious mechanisms. adj. **diseased**.

disorderly conduct An offense, sometimes defined by statute, disturbing to the morals, safety, or peace of the public.

dissolution of marriage The legal termination of marriage by divorce, i.e. a severance of the marriage bond itself. See **annulment, divorce**.

divorce n. The legal termination of a marriage by court decree or judgment. See **annulment, dissolution of marriage**.

DNA (deoxyribonucleic acid) The molecule that contains basic genetic material, or genes, within a chromosome.

dominant gene One of a pair of genes that can manifest itself in the presence of a more recessive gene. See **recessive gene**.

dose n. Slang for gonorrhea.

douche n. A jet of fluid directed on or into a body part for a medicinal or hygienic purpose; commonly, a vaginal douche.

doxycycline n. An antibiotic of the tetracycline group used in the treatment of prostatitis and pelvic inflammatory disease (PID).

drip n. Slang for gonorrhea.

drug n. A substance taken as medication to combat a microorganism or to alter the function of the body; a substance that causes addiction.

dyspepsia See **indigestion**.

eclampsia n. A disease state, caused by unknown toxins, marked by high blood pressure and convulsions during pregnancy .

ectopic pregnancy A fertilized ovum developing outside the uterus.

ego n. In Freudian psychology, the part of the psyche which organizes rational thought and controls action. See **id, psyche, superego**.

ejaculation n. The discharge of a fluid; esp. the discharge of semen in a male orgasm. v. **ejaculate**.

elective abortion An abortion not needed to protect the health of the mother and which she elects to have performed to end a pregnancy. See **abortion**.

element n. A substance that cannot be separated into constituent parts by chemical reaction and which is composed of like atoms.

emancipation n. The attainment of freedom or legal majority; the act effecting freedom, e.g. a parent's surrender of all parental rights emancipates a child.

embryo n. The early development of a fertilized ovum, before becoming a fetus, from about two weeks after fertilization until the seventh or eighth week of gestation.

encephalitis n. Inflammation of the brain usually caused by a viral infection.

endocrine adj. Pertaining to a gland that releases its secretion inside the gland itself, e.g. the thyroid gland; such a gland is also called a ductless gland.

endometriosis n. The occurrence of tissue like the lining of the uterus in locations where such tissue is not normally found, e.g. in the pelvic cavity outside the uterus.

endometritis n. Inflammation of the lining of the uterus, usually caused by a bacterial infection.

endometrium n. The mucous membrane lining of the uterus.

enzyme n. One of many specific proteins that as a group regulate the rates of bodily chemical reactions, e.g. lipase is produced by the pancreas to aid in digestion.

epididymis n. A cordlike or tubular mass on the back surface of a testicle (testis).

epididymitis n. Painful swelling and inflammation of the epididymis, often producing chills and fever.

equilibrium n. A balance of body forces necessary for physiologic function.

equitable distribution The distribution of property, deemed by the court to be just, between husband and wife upon divorce or dissolution of marriage.

equity n. Justice, administered by principles of fairness, rather than by strict or rigid rules of law. adj. **equitable.**

erogenous adj. Pertaining to sexual arousal; esp. to areas of the body where stimulation encourages such arousal.

erythromycin n. An antibiotic drug used in the treatment of skin, chest, throat, ear, and genital infections.

esophagus n. The canal through which food passes from the pharynx to the stomach.

estate n. Property, real or personal, owned by a person; the kind of interest owned in such property.

estrogen n. The female sex hormone, produced in the ovaries, that produces conditions favorable for fertilization of the ovum and early embryonic development; found in small quantities in males. See **progesterone.**

eugenic sterilization Sterilization to improve a race's hereditary qualities, esp. by preventing the passing of some undesirable trait.

excision n. The surgical removal of a body part.

excretion n. A substance separated and eliminated from the body as useless or even harmful. See **secretion.**

exocrine adj. Pertaining to a gland that releases its secretion outside the gland itself through a duct, e.g. a tear gland, a sweat gland.

exploitation n. The act of utilizing or of taking unjust advantage of another for one's own benefit.

extracellular adj. Occurring outside a cell.

eye n. An organ of sight contained at the front of the skull in a bony orbit or socket.

eyebrow n. The ridge over the orbit or socket of the eye, or the hair on the ridge.

eyelash n. One of the cilia (hairs) growing on the edge of the eyelid.

factor n. An element that influences a result.

Fahrenheit adj. A scale for measuring temperature that fixes the freezing point of water at 32 degrees above zero, and the boiling point of water at 212 degrees above zero; abbreviated F (compare centigrade).

Fallopian tube One of two tubes transporting the egg or ovum from the ovary to the uterus. See **oviduct, salpinx.**

familial adj. Characteristic of, or common to, a family; sometimes congenital or hereditary.

fault n. A failing; a wrongful act; something subject to blame.

FDA Food and Drug Administration. An agency of the U.S. Department of Health and Human Services charged with the responsibility of approving drugs for prescription use and other related responsibilities, such as approval of foods, cosmetics, and medical devices.

fear n. Dread of harm; apprehension.

feces n. Bodily waste discharged from the bowel in defecation. adj. **fecal.**

fellatio n. Stimulation of the penis, orally.

felony n. A serious crime punishable, as prescribed by statute, by imprisonment or even death. See **misdemeanor.**

fertile adj. Capable of conceiving, that is, of becoming pregnant if female, or of impregnating if male. n. **fertility.**

fetus n. The developing child-to-be, in the uterus, subsequent to the embryonic period. adj. **fetal.**

fetus abuse Failure of the mother-to-be during pregnancy, to provide the fetus with protective prenatal care, appropriate nutrition, and the like. See **abuse.**

fever n. Temperature of the body above normal.

fimbria n. An edge, border, or fringe. pl. **fimbriae.**

Flagyl n. The trade name of a drug (metronidazole) used to treat certain protozoan infections including trichomonal vaginitis.

Food and Drug Administration See **FDA.**

forensic adj. Suitable for court proceedings.

foreskin n. The folded skin covering the glans of the penis; also known as the prepuce.

fornication n. Voluntary sexual intercourse between two unmarried persons; or if between a married and an unmarried person, sometimes the former is considered to be an adulterer and the latter a fornicator. See **adultery**.

fraud n. An artifice intended to deceive; perversion of truth to injure another.

frustration n. The prevention of the gratification of one's impulses or desires.

fungus n. Any of the lower plants or organisms lacking chlorophyll, such as molds, mildews and yeasts, some of which cause disease; also, a slang term for fungal vaginitis. pl. **fungi**, adj. **fungal**.

gall See **bile**.

gallbladder A reservoir for bile, or gall, located on the under surface of the right side of the liver.

Gardnerella vaginalis A bacterium that causes nonspecific vaginitis.

garnishment n. The statutory process whereby the disposition of a person's property, such as wages, is held subject to the order of a court.

GC n. Slang for gonorrhea.

gene n. A segment of a DNA molecule which determines and transmits hereditary characteristics; the fundamental biological unit of heredity. adj. **genetic**. See **dominant gene, recessive gene**.

generic drug A drug without a brand or trademarked name.

genetic father The male whose sperm fertilizes an ovum.

genetic mother The female from whose fertilized ovum a fetus develops.

genital herpes A painful viral infection occurring in the genital area.

genital tract The region of the body containing parts related to the reproductive process; the genitals.

genital wart A viral evoked tumor on the male or female genitals.

genitalia n. The reproductive organs of males and females. adj. **genital**, pl. **genitals**.

germ n. A disease-producing microorganism.

gestation n. The time beginning with fertilization of the ovum and ending with the birth of a child.

gift n. The voluntary conveyance of the ownership of property to another without consideration.

gland n. An organ that produces a secretion or excretion needed in other parts of the body; e.g. an endocrine gland secretes hormones, an exocrine gland releases sweat, tears, etc.

glans clitoris The head of the clitoris.

glans penis The head of the penis.

gleet n. Slang for gonorrhea.

globulin n. A group of proteins of immunologic function, found in the blood.

gonad n. The organ that generates reproductive cells; testicle (testis) or ovary.

gonococcus n. The extracellular bacterium (Neisseria gonorrhoeae) that is the cause of gonorrhea. adj. **gonococcal** pl. **gonococci.**

gonorrhea n. A venereal disease initially affecting the urethra and vagina, but which if untreated will lead to widespread infections and disorders, especially in females.

granuloma inguinale A chronic and progressive venereal disease caused by a bacterial infection, and characterized by ulcers in the genital and groin regions.

griseofulvin n. An antibiotic taken orally in the treatment of fungal infections, particularly of the skin and nails.

groin n. The space between the thigh and the lower abdomen.

guardian ad litem A court appointee to act on behalf of a minor, or an incompetent adult, in connection with a suit.

Gyne-Lotrimin n. The trade name of clotrimazole.

Haemophilus ducreyi The bacterium that causes chancroid.

haircut n. Slang for syphilis.

hang-up n. Slang; a difficult problem, esp. an emotional one that is hard to resolve.

having sex Participating in any form of sexual activity, free from injury, pain, or physical damage. See **sex.**

HBIG (hepatitis B immune globulin) n. An immunizing protein injected to provide temporary immunity from contracting hepatitis B.

HBV (hepatitis B virus) A virus that causes a specific liver inflammation.

headache n. Pain occurring in the head.

heart n. The organ that acts as a pump to force the circulation of the blood throughout the body.

heartburn n. A burning sensation below the breast area caused by a backflow of stomach acid into the esophagus.

heir n. A person entitled to inherit property under a statutory law of descent and distribution; or, more loosely, one who inherits by either will or statute. See **statutory heir.**

hemoglobin n. A molecular compound present in red blood cells, which carries oxygen to body tissues and carbon dioxide from body tissues.

hemophilia n. An inherited blood disorder, usually manifest in males, and characterized by a tendency towards excessive bleeding.

hemophiliac n. One who has hemophilia.

hemorrhage n. The profuse and rapid discharge of blood, externally or internally.

hepatitis n. An inflammation of the liver, often severe, sometimes fatal.

hepatitis B immune globulin See **HBIG.**

hepatitis B vaccine A suspension of altered or killed microorganisms administered to give immunity to hepatitis B.

hepatitis B virus See **HBV.**

hereditary adj. Passed down or transmitted from parents to offspring, commonly a genetic trait. See **congenital, familial.**

herpes n. A virus infection that causes a painful blistering of the skin or mucous membranes.

herpes simplex Type 1 A herpes virus that usually infects the eye or facial area.

herpes simplex Type 2 A herpes virus that usually infects the genital area.

heterosexual n. A person who engages in, or is oriented toward, sexual activity with another of the opposite sex.

heterosexuality n. Sexual behavior between persons of the opposite sex.

HIV (human immunodeficiency virus) The AIDS virus; a retrovirus that invades body cells, spreads and multiplies, to weaken the body's immune system.

hives n. Urticaria; a skin disorder with itchy wheals, or elevated red blotches.

HLA (human leukocyte antigen) One of an inherited group of proteins present naturally in tissue and functioning in the body's immune system.

HLA testing A method of determining paternity by which tissue samples from mother, child, and possible father are examined for commonly held genetic markers.

homicide n. The killing of one human by another. Statutory degrees of homicide generally include murder, manslaughter, or negligent homicide.

homosexual n. A person who engages in or is oriented toward, sexual activity with another of the same sex. A lesbian is a female homosexual. See lesbian.

homosexuality n. Sexual behavior between persons of the same sex.

hormone n. A complex substance (created naturally by specific glands or synthetically) which is carried by body fluids and which regulates the activity of specific organs or tissues. See estrogen, progesterone, testosterone.

HPV (human papilloma virus) The microorganism that causes genital warts.

HTLV III (human T cell lymphotropic virus III) The virus that causes AIDS; now referred to as HIV.

human leukocyte antigen See HLA.

human papilloma virus See HPV.

human T cell lymphotropic virus III See HTLV III.

hydramnios n. An excessive amount of amniotic fluid around the fetus, in pregnancy.

hypertension n. Persistent, abnormally high arterial blood pressure; also, the systemic condition that accompanies high blood pressure. adj. hypertensive

hypochondria n. Abnormal concern for one's health, sometimes accompanied by imaginary illness and melancholy.

hysterectomy n. Surgical excision of the uterus; removal of the ovaries (oophorectomy) may be done at the same time.

hysterotomy n. The surgical cutting of the uterus, particularly as done for Cesarean section.

id n. In Freudian psychology, the unconscious part of the psyche providing instincts and drives, such as the instinctive avoidance of pain and the drive, often irrational, to pursue pleasure. See **ego, psyche, superego.**

illegitimate adj. Unlawful; with reference to a child, a child whose parents were never married to each other or were not married to each other at the time of conception, the time of birth, or after the birth of the child. See **bastard, legitimate.**

immune adj. Highly resistant to or protected from a disease, esp. an infectious one. n. **immunity.** See **acquired immunity.**

immune globulin An extract of antibodies from blood or serum used to provide immunity, often temporary, against some diseases, or to treat immunodeficient patients.

immunodeficiency n. A lacking of the body's antibody system to fight infections and tumors.

impotence n. Inability of a male or female to engage in sexual intercourse; to be distinguished from sterility, which is inability to become a parent. adj. **impotent.** See **sterility.**

in utero Inside the uterus.

in vitro Inside glass; under laboratory conditions.

in vivo Inside the body.

incapacity n. Incapability; inability to act legally. See **mental incompetent.**

incest n. Criminal incest means sexual intercourse between persons within the prohibited degrees of relationship by blood, adoption, or marriage; civil incest is attempted marriage between a male and a female within the degrees of relationship by blood or marriage specified in each state's laws concerning capacity to marry. adj. **incestuous.**

incidence n. The number or rate of occurrences in a specified period of time. See **prevalence.**

incompetency n. Unfitness; lack of qualification for legal action. See **mental incompetent.**

incompetent cervix Premature dilation of the exit opening of the uterus, without labor, before term, in pregnancy.

incomplete miscarriage See **miscarriage.**

incubation period The time between infection and the first symptom of a disease.

indecent exposure The indictable exhibition, in a lewd manner or in a public place, of the body's private parts.

indict v. To accuse in legal proceedings of a fault or offense. n. **indictment.**

indigestion n. A gastric or alimentary disorder characterized by nausea, heartburn, or upset stomach; dyspepsia.

induced abortion An abortion which is accomplished by medical or surgical means; one may be elective, when the health of the mother is not in danger, or therapeutic, when the health of the mother is in danger. See **abortion.**

induced labor The stimulation of childbirth by artificial means such as drugs or surgery.

inevitable miscarriage See **miscarriage.**

infect v. To transmit a disease to a receptive host. n. **infector.**

infection n. A disease caused by the invasion of a pathogen (that is, a disease producing microorganism) into the body.

infectious adj. Capable of communicating a pathogenic organism.

infective adj. Infectious.

infertile adj. Not capable of conceiving after a year of trying by intercourse. n. **infertility.**

infertility n. Inability to impregnate (male) or to conceive (female); sterility. adj. **infertile.**

infestation n. An increasing swarm of parasites on or in the body.

inflammation n. The localized swelling, redness, heat, and pain of body tissues responding to irritation, infection, or injury.

injection n. The act of forcing a substance into the body by syringe; the substance so forced. v. **inject.**

insanity n. A broad term for mental disorders arising from a number of different, specific causes; also, the degree of mental derangement sufficient to negate legal capacity.

inseminate v. To introduce semen or sperm into the vagina. n. **insemination.**

insulin n. A protein hormone that helps regulate the body's use of sugar; a drug made from hormones and used in the treatment of diabetes mellitus.

intent n. The purpose or aim involved in an action; the mental attitude of the person committing an act.

intercourse n. Contact, usually verbal, between persons or groups; a sexual coupling between male and female. See **sexual intercourse.**

interferon n. An antiviral protein that works by stimulating a host to activity against viruses.

intestacy n. Being or dying without a will. adj. **intestate.**

intestine n. The canal, divided into two parts, extending from the stomach to the anus. Digestion occurs in the small intestine; and, after absorbing water, the residues of digestion are eliminated from the large intestine.

intracellular adj. Occurring within a cell.

intrauterine contraceptive device See **IUD.**

intravenous See **IV.**

invalid adj. Lacking in legal force; void.

iron n. A common metallic chemical element, necessary for life.

irrigation n. The flushing of a body part by a liquid such as water.

itch n. An irritation of the skin causing a desire to scratch.

-itis A noun suffix meaning inflammation; e.g. prostatitis means inflammation of the prostate.

IUD (intrauterine contraceptive device) A small piece, variously shaped, of metal or plastic, used as an insertion into the uterus through the vagina, for continuous contraception. Also called IUD, intrauterine loop, intrauterine coil, intrauterine device.

IV (intravenous) Into a vein; an intravenous injection.

jaundice n. The yellowing of the skin and of the whites of the eyes because of an increase in bile pigments.

joint tenants Usually two persons owning an interest in the same property; e.g. a husband and wife often own their residence as joint tenants. In most but not all places such property will be held by the survivor. See **tenant**.

judgment n. Mental ability to comprehend and to form an opinion; a court's decision or order; a debt incurred by court order.

Kaposi's sarcoma A cancerous or malignant tumor which usually spreads from the skin to internal organs, and which is a common complication of AIDS.

kidney n. One of two bean-shaped organs located in the back of the abdominal cavity that filters the blood and excretes waste and water as urine.

Kwell n. Trade name of an insecticide (lindane) used to treat infestations of lice and mites by application to the skin.

labium n. A fleshy edge or border; esp. the large outer and small inner edges of the female external genitalia. pl. **labia.**

labor n. The process of the female by which the products of conception are expelled from the uterus. It is frequently divided into three stages: dilation, expulsion, and placenta or afterbirth.

laxative n. A medicine promoting a looseness of the bowels to relieve constipation; a cathartic.

legal adj. Lawful; permitted or created by law.

legitimate adj. Lawful; of a child born to married parents. See **illegitimate**.

lesbian n. A female homosexual. See **homosexual**.

lesion n. A general term for a local tissue abnormality, such as a wound, boil, sore, tumor, or the like.

leukocyte n. A white blood cell that is important as part of the defense mechanism of the body.

levonorgestrel n. A synthetic progesterone, the female sex hormone that assists the pregnancy process in the uterus.

levy v. To inaugurate; to collect; to assess or exact a tax or a fine; to attach by court order.

liability n. A hazard; a legal obligation such as a debt.

libido n. The sexual urge or drive; a basic psychic force involving loving instincts which vary at different stages of personal development.

ligament n. A tough connecting tissue, binding bones or organs.

ligation n. A tie or bind to block the passage of material through a body part such as a vessel or duct. v. **ligate.**

lindane n. An insecticide. See **Kwell.**

liquid diet n. A schedule of food in the form of liquids or jellies.

liver n. The large glandular organ located in the upper right side of the abdominal cavity, which performs many complex body functions including the excretion of bile, the regulation of blood sugar, the detoxification of poisonous substances, and the production of plasma proteins.

lotion n. A liquid preparation used externally to soothe, or to heal, disorders of the skin.

louse n. A small, flat insect, parasitic on man and/or other mammals, with a sucking mouth. pl. **lice.** See **crab louse.**

lues n. Another name for syphilis.

lung n. One of the two respiratory organs, located in the chest, that inhales air, takes out oxygen, and exhales carbon dioxide.

Lyme disease A disease caused by spirochetes similar to the syphilis spirochete, transmitted by certain ticks, causing a skin rash, fever, and headache initially, and, possibly, arthritis, eye, and heart damage later.

lymph n. A collected, yellowish tissue fluid similar to plasma, containing white blood cells, that circulates through lymph nodes into the blood stream.

lymph node A small cluster (normally 1 to 25 mm in size) of germinal cells which give rise to white blood cells and the body's cellular defenses.

lymphocyte n. A white blood cell, part of the body's system of resistance against infections and diseases.

lymphogranuloma venereum A venereal disease caused by an infection with the bacterium Chlamydia trachomatis, and characterized by headache, fever, malaise, swelling of lymph nodes in the groin, and genital lesions.

majority n. More than half; legal age; the age at which by law a person is old enough to manage affairs. See **adult, minority.**

malaise n. A feeling of uneasiness often preceding the onset of illness.

malignant adj. Deadly; esp. a cancer that spreads and terminates in death.

marriage n. The contract between one man and one woman to become united by law, with or without religious ceremony, as husband and wife. The bond of marriage created by a valid contract can be dissolved only by the death of a party or by divorce (order of a court). See **annulment, divorce, dissolution of marriage.**

masochism n. Derivation of sexual gratification by being humiliated or physically hurt by another.

masturbation n. The manual stimulation of the genitals, by one's self or by another, for purposes of sexual gratification.

medication n. A drug, lotion, balm, salve, ointment, or other remedy used for curing disorders or for relieving pain.

membrane n. A thin sheet of connective tissue that lines body parts. See **mucous membrane**.

meninges n. The three membranes that envelope and protect the brain and the spinal cord. sing. **menix**.

meningitis n. Inflammation of the meninges caused by any one of a number of infections or irritations.

menopause n. The permanent, natural stoppage of menstrual periods.

menses See **menstruation**.

menstrual cycle The recurring 28-day cycle of ovarian and uterine function.

menstrual flow The flow of blood during menstruation.

menstruation n. The periodic discharge of blood and tissue from the uterus through the vagina; menses; usually the "period" occurs at approximately four week intervals. adj. **menstrual**.

mental incompetent A person lacking the mental capacity to act responsibly for him or herself. See **incompetency**.

mental retardation Mental deficiency, or impaired intellectual capability, inhibiting the ability to function normally in life.

metabolism n. The physical and chemical bodily processes whereby nutrients are absorbed, energy is generated, and wastes are eliminated.

metronidazole See **Flagyl**.

miconazole nitrate A synthetic antifungal agent effective against several fungi.

microbe n. A minute, living organism that is visible only with a microscope.

microorganism n. A unicellular, living organism, e.g. a bacterium, virus, fungus, or protozoon.

mifepristone n. An anti-progesterone. See **RU 486**.

minor n. A person not an adult, who has not attained the age of legal majority (which is 18 in nearly all states) or been emancipated by marriage or legal process; in legal language, a minor is a "child" until majority. adj. **minor**

minority n. Less than half; the age of a person before reaching majority. See **adult, majority**.

miscarriage n. The involuntary early expulsion of a fetus before it can survive outside of the uterus or womb. There are incomplete, inevitable, missed, and threatened miscarriages. Miscarriages are known medically as spontaneous abortions. See **abortion**.

misdemeanor n. An offense less serious than a felony, generally punishable by a fine or short term imprisonment. See **felony**.

missed miscarriage See **miscarriage**.

mite n. Any of a group of small insects (related to spiders and ticks), some of which can irritate or burrow within the skin.

molecule n. The smallest particle of a substance that exists alone, and which is a combination of two or more atoms. adj. **molecular**.

molluscum n. A disease of the skin, usually appearing in round, soft masses.

moniliasis n. Candidiasis; an infection caused by Candida albicans, a species of fungus, commonly of the vagina and male urethra.

Monistat 7 n. The trade name of miconazole nitrate.

monogamy n. Marriage with but one person at a time. adj. **monogamous.**

mons pubis The rounded prominence in the lower female abdomen just above the external genitalia. Also called **mons veneris.**

mons veneris See **mons pubis.**

mores n. pl. Generally observed customs considered to be good for society and which often become incorporated into the law.

morning sickness An urge to vomit, particularly in the early hours of the day, common in pregnancies, .

mucopurulent adj. Having the characteristics of a mixture of mucus and pus.

mucous membrane A smooth, lubricating liner or surface connective tissue of body passages and cavities, that protects organs and secretes mucus.

mucus n. Viscid secretions of the mucous membrane. adj. **mucous.**

mycoplasma n. A class or group of very small bacteria, some of which cause disease in humans; e.g. mycoplasma pneumonia.

nasal adj. Relating to the nose.

nausea n. An uncomfortable feeling with impaired balance and an urge to vomit.

navel n. The place in the abdominal wall where the umbilical cord was attached; the "bellybutton."

negligence n. Failure to use reasonable care; conduct below legal protective standards.

Neisseria gonorrhoeae See gonococcus.

neonate n. A newborn during the first month of its life. adj. **neonatal.**

neurosyphilis n. Infection of the nervous system by the spirochete that is the cause of syphilis; commonly the third stage of syphilis.

neurotic n. A person suffering from any of several functional mental disorders involving anxiety, depression, phobia, etc. adj. **neurotic.**

newborn n. A recently born baby.

nicotine n. A toxic substance present in tobacco, believed to cause dependence on tobacco by smokers.

nipple n. A sensitive protuberance on the breast; in females, it emits milk for a suckling infant.

nocturnal emission See **wet dream.**

nocturnal orgasm A female orgasm induced by an erotic dream.

node n. A small cluster of cells, usually similar or related in function.

nonoxynol-9 n. A chemical that is used as a spermicide.

nonspecific infection An infection, often of the genitalia, caused by a microorganism that is neither Neisseria gonorrhoeae nor Chlamydia trachomatis.

nonspecific urethritis Inflammation of the urethra caused by an unidentified organism.

nontherapeutic sterilization Sterilization for reasons other than medical treatment, i.e. so as not to have children.

Norplant n. The trade name of levonorgestrel.

nourishment n. Food necessary to sustain life. v. **nourish**.

nucleus n. The center of a structure, a roughly spherical structure, within a cell, around which is the cytoplasm. It is the location of chromosomes and their vital DNA.

obscenity n. Lewdness; an offense against accepted standards of decency. In U.S. constitutional law, material which is obscene falls outside the protections of the First Amendment (free speech) and thus can be forbidden by law. adj. **obscene**.

odor n. A scent stimulating the sense of smell by direct chemical contact.

ointment n. A salve for application to the skin or mucous membranes for cosmetic, or, if medicated, for healing purposes.

old joe Slang for syphilis.

oophorectomy n. The excision of one or both ovaries.

opportunistic infection An infection caused, in a human, by an organism which does not normally cause infection but which can do so as a result of a badly functioning immune system.

oral adj. Relating to the mouth.

oral sex A phrase increasingly in use, referring, apparently, to any form of sexual stimulation by means of the mouth or tongue, but without injury or pain.

organ n. A body part having a specific function such as the heart or lungs.

organic adj. All chemical compounds containing carbon; or relating to body organs; or to a change in a body organ.

organism n. Any form of life such as an animal or a plant, and, microscopically, a cell, bacterium, virus, or the like.

orgasm n. The climax of sexual excitement achieved by sexual intercourse; or by other sexual stimulation such as masturbation or erotic dreams.

ovary n. One of two female reproductive organs that produce ova, or eggs; gonad. adj. **ovarian**.

oviduct n. The tube or duct through which the ova passes. See **Fallopian tube, salpinx**.

ovulation n. The escape, sometimes painful, of an egg (ovum) from the ovary, normally into one of the Fallopian tubes.

ovum n. Egg; the female reproductive cell that may unite with a single sperm cell in fertilization. pl. **ova**.

oxygenated adj. Combined with oxygen.

oxytetracycline n. An antibiotic used to treat chlamydial infections.

pain n. A hurting sensation transmitted by sensory nerves to the brain.

palimony n. An award or settlement of property arising from a nonmarital relationship.

palpitation n. A rapid or fluttering heart-beat caused by emotion or excessive stimulation.

pander or panderer n. A prostitute's solicitor; a pimp; a go-between in sexual scheming.

Pap smear or Pap test See **Papanicolaou test**.

Papanicolaou test A test for the early detection of cancer by the examination of stained cells from mucous membranes, particularly cells from the mucous membrane of the cervix. (Papanicolaou was an American physician.)

paralysis n. Loss, complete or partial, of muscle function in a part of the body. pl. **paralyses**, adj. **paralytic**.

parenthood n. Becoming the mother or father of a child.

pediculosis pubis The formal name of an infestation of crab lice.

Pediculus pubis The louse that infests pubic hair, causing pediculosis pubis, which is also known as crab lice.

pejorative adj. Disparaging; making worse, esp. relative to words having had their meanings changed for the worse.

pelvic inflammatory disease (PID) An inflamed condition of the female reproductive organs and adjacent structures, often a result of bacterial infection.

pelvis n. The cavity in the lower part of the trunk of the body between the right and left hip bones, protecting the lower abdominal organs. adj. **pelvic**.

penicillin n. Any of several antibiotics produced synthetically or by molds, used to treat many bacterial infections.

penis n. The male organ of copulation and urination, through which semen (in orgasm) and urine pass; it contains three columns of erectile tissue. adj. **penile**.

perinatal adj. Concerning the period of time shortly before and after birth.

perineum n. Commonly, the space between the anus and the vulva in females, or between the anus and the scrotum in males.

period n. The periodic flow of blood and tissue during menstruation. See **menses, menstrual cycle, menstrual flow, menstruation**.

peritoneum n. The smooth membrane that lines the cavity of the abdomen and that envelopes the abdominal organs.

peritonitis n. Inflammation of the peritoneum resulting from bacteria, other microorganisms, or irritating foreign matter.

pharynx n. The passageway used by food to go from the mouth to the esophagus.

phobia n. An irrational, intense fear of some object, situation, or condition; e.g. zoophobia is an abnormal fear of dogs, cats, or other animals.

photosensitivity n. Abnormal sensitivity or reaction to sunlight or similar ultraviolet and other light sources.

photosynthesis n. The creation of carbohydrates by combination of water and carbon dioxide with release of oxygen, under the influence of light in chlorophyll-containing plants. adj. **photosynthetic**.

PID See **pelvic inflammatory disease**.

pill n. A medicine in the form of a small tablet, capsule, or the like, to be swallowed whole.

pimp n. A procurer for a prostitute; a panderer.

placenta n. The organ that develops within the pregnant uterus to provide nourishment for the fetus and the elimination of wastes during gestation. The placenta is expelled in the third stage of labor and is therefore sometimes called afterbirth.

placenta previa A placenta abnormally and dangerously developing in the uterus, sometimes obstructing the passage from the uterus to the vagina.

plaintiff n. A person who sues in a civil action; the state's prosecutor in a criminal case. See **defendant**.

Planned Parenthood Federation A national organization with many local affiliates which provide confidential contraceptive advice and materials, infertility and abortion counseling, and, in some locations abortion services.

plaque n. An abnormal raised patch on a part of the body; also a deposit on the teeth.

plasma n. The part of blood, lymph, and milk that is fluid, as distinguished from circulating cells or suspended matter.

platelet n. The cellular element of the blood, essential for blood clotting.

pneumococcus n. A bacterium that frequently causes pneumonia or inflammation of the lungs. pl. **pneumococci.**

pneumonia n. An inflammatory disease of the lungs caused by infection with pneumococci or other microorganisms, or by other irritants.

podophyllin n. A resin used as a topical caustic in the treatment of genital warts.

pornographic adj. Obscene; appealing to prurient interests by community standards. Recently, pornographic has been used to mean material which is degrading to women; such material may or may not be legally obscene. n. **pornography.**

postmature baby n. A baby born after 42 weeks of gestation, 38 weeks being normal.

postpartum hemorrhage A bleeding, usually from the uterus or vagina, occurring within a few days after childbirth.

pox n. Any one of various diseases characterized by skin pustules or blisters, such as chicken pox and smallpox; also, an older reference to syphilis, or the "great pox."

pre-eclampsia n. A toxic condition during pregnancy of unknown cause, which may lead to eclampsia (convulsions) with the risk of both child and maternal death.

pregnancy n. The time from conception to the birth of a child.

pregnant adj. Having a developing child within the female body.

premature adj. Happening ahead of the normal time.

premature delivery The birth of a baby before 38 weeks of gestation during a pregnancy.

premature ejaculation Ejaculation and loss of erection that occurs before or shortly after penetration of the vagina by the penis, usually in younger males.

premature labor Uterine contraction occurring before the 38th week of normal pregnancy.

prenatal adj. Previous to birth.

prenatal testing Diagnostic examinations of several types to identify fetal abnormalities.

prepuce n. The fold of skin that in males covers the glans of the penis, and in females surrounds the clitoris.

prescription drug A drug available only with a medical prescription.

prevalence n. The number of events occurring during a specified period of time; or the number of events (such as the number of cases of a disease) existing at a particular time. See **incidence.**

primary adj. Of the first stage, order, rank, etc.; first.

privacy n. The right of an individual to information of a personal nature; the right of a person to be let alone.

procurer n. A person who procures sexual gratification for another; one who brings something about corruptly.

progesterone n. The female sex hormone that assists and promotes the pregnancy process in the uterus; the principal pregnancy hormone. See **estrogen, RU 486.**

promiscuity n. Frequent, indiscriminate, and careless sexual activity, which statistically enhances the chance of contracting a disease or having an unwanted pregnancy. adj. **promiscuous.**

prophylactic n. A disease-preventive measure or medicine; e.g. a condom. adj. **prophylactic.**

prophylaxis n. Measures to prevent a disease, or the spread of disease.

prostaglandin n. A class of hormone-like chemicals useful in the treatment of various diseases, including reproductive disorders. See **RU 486.**

prostate gland A glandular organ in the male located at the base of the bladder and at the neck of the urethra, that produces the fluid part of semen; often called simply prostate.

prostatitis n. Inflammation of the prostate gland, usually by infection, and causing fever and chills, as well as pain and frequent urination.

prostitution n. The act of selling, or offering to sell, sexual engagements.

protein n. Any one of a group of complex compounds of amino acids that are essential for life processes.

protozoon n. Any of a certain group of microorganisms consisting of a single cell; some of the group cause disease. pl. **protozoa.**

psyche n. The mind, based on physical aspects of the brain but including complex mental functions of its own; it controls the body and its actions related to the environment; in Freudian psychology, the total of the ego, id, and superego. See **ego, id, superego.**

psychiatry n. The medical specialty that deals with mental disorders, esp. the study, treatment, and prevention thereof.

psychic adj. Pertaining to the mind or psyche, rather than to the physical.

psychogenic adj. Of mental rather than physical origin, or resulting from mental conflicts.

psychology n. The science relating to the human and animal minds and their emotional, as well as mental, processes and behavior. adj. **psychological.**

psychopath n. One who suffers from a disorder of the mind causing antisocial, or even criminal, behavior.

psychosexual adj. Relating to the psychological, rather than the physical, aspects of sexual behavior.

psychosis n. A serious mental disorder, often requiring hospitalization, involving personality disorganization and impairment of contact with reality.

psychotherapy n. The remedial psychological rather than physical treatment of a mental disorder, provided by counseling, psycho-analysis, etc.

psychotic n. A person suffering from psychosis. adj. **psychotic.**

puberty n. The period in the growth of the male and female when sexual reproduction becomes possible; among other noticeable changes, the male voice deepens and female menstruation begins.

pubescent adj. Having arrived at puberty.

pubic lice See crab lice.

pubis n. One of two corresponding bones that meet at the front of the pelvis. pl. **pubes.** adj. **pubic.**

public indecency A vague phrase, legally; loosely, acts of nakedness or obscenity which, in the judgment of a court, offend public morals.

public nuisance Anything or anybody hurting or damaging the health or welfare of the public.

public place A site which the general public uses to gather in or to pass through.

punitive damages Damages awarded as punishment for outrageous behavior in excess of compensation for injury to person or property. See **damages.**

pus n. A yellow-white fluid occurring at an infection site, containing tissue debris, dead white blood cells, and bacteria.

pustule n. A blister-like elevation of the skin containing pus. adj. **pustular.**

rape n. The crime of sexual intercourse with another by force or without the other's consent, perhaps because the other is below the minimum age specified for consent. See **age of consent, child abuse, consent, statutory rape.**

rash n. An eruption of the skin usually consisting of red spots or areas.

reaction n. The body's response to a drug, medical treatment, antigen, or the like.

recessive gene One of a pair of genes that cannot manifest itself in the presence of a more dominant gene; e.g. a gene for blue eyes cannot express itself in the presence of a dominant gene for brown eyes. See **dominant gene.**

rectum n. The terminal portion of the large intestine in which feces are stored before defecation, connecting the colon and the anus. adj. **rectal.**

regimen n. A regulated program of diet, exercise, etc., designed to maintain or improve health.

Reiter's syndrome A chronic disorder, usually in males, normally beginning with diarrhea and followed by conjunctivitis, urethritis, and arthritis.

remedy n. A cure; redress; the legal means of enforcing a right or of preventing the violation of a right.

resistance n. The extent of immunity from a disease possessed by a human body; the extent to which a microorganism is unaffected by medication; e.g. the extent to which bacteria are resistant to penicillin.

respiratory distress syndrome An acute lung disorder, esp. of a premature baby, which makes breathing difficult and inadequate.

retarded adj. Slow in development, esp. in mental growth.

retina n. The inner layer of the eyeball that transmits visual stimuli to the optic nerve and to the brain.

Retrovir n. The trade name of AZT (zidovudine).

retrovirus n. A member of a large group of minute infectious agents that cause AIDS, degenerative brain diseases, and, perhaps, some cancers.

Rh factor An inherited antigen occurring in the blood of most persons, first discovered in the blood of the Rhesus monkey. Such persons are said to be Rh positive. Persons whose blood does not have such an element are classified as Rh negative. If Rh negative persons receive Rh positive blood in a transfusion, severe consequences follow. Similar consequences can affect an Rh negative mother if her fetus is Rh positive.

Rh negative See **Rh factor.**

Rh positive See **Rh factor.**

rheumatic fever A serious, painful, inflammatory disease, usually preceded by a sore throat, typically occurring in children, sometimes with cardiac involvement.

right of privacy See **privacy.**

Rocephin n The trade name of a broad spectrum antibiotic used to treat gonorrhea; ceftriaxone.

RU 486 Mifepristone; an anti-progesterone. A German drug used in "self" abortions, available in France, but not FDA-approved in the United States. In France, in the early days of pregnancy, a female may take three small doses of RU 486 and, later, an injection of prostaglandin, and in almost all cases, the fertilized egg will be sloughed off the wall of the uterus in a private, "self-induced" abortion.

rubber n. Slang for condom.

rupture n. A tear or breach.

sac n. A thin walled, pouch-like organ; esp. one containing a fluid.

sadism n. Pleasure derived from the infliction of mental or physical pain on another, esp. sexual sadism.

safe Slang for condom.

saliva n. The secretion of the glands draining into the mouth that aids the tasting, chewing, and digestion of food. adj. **salivary**.

salpingitis n. Infection of a Fallopian tube (salpinx or oviduct), usually having spread from the vagina or uterus.

salpinx n. A tube, e.g. a Fallopian tube. See **oviduct**.

salt n. A chemical compound formed by an acid neutralized by a base, esp. sodium chloride, or "table salt."

salve n. An ointment for application to the skin for cosmetic, or, if medicated, for healing purposes.

sarcoma n. A malignant tumor whose cells resemble connective tissue, muscle, or bone.

Sarcoptes scabiei The mite that causes scabies.

scab n. The hardened crust that forms over a healing wound.

scabies n. A contagious, itching skin disease caused by a burrowing mite, Sarcoptes scabiei.

scar n. Cicatrix; the new tissue left after the healing of a wound, burn, lesion, ulcer, etc.

sciatic nerve n. The nerve between the thigh and the knee.

sciatica n. A pain from the thigh down the leg, esp. pain in the area of the sciatic nerve.

scrotum n. The sac of skin attached under the penis and containing principally the testes.

secondary adj. Of the second stage, order, rank, etc.; second.

secretion n. A substance such as saliva or perspiration, separated, elaborated, and released from the blood or body organs. See **excretion**.

sedative n. A medicine having a calming and relaxing effect.

seduce v. To lead astray; to induce, esp. the chaste, to have sexual intercourse.

self breast-test See **breast examination**.

semen n. The fluid, derived primarily from the testicles and prostate gland, discharged in ejaculation, that contains male sex cells (spermatozoa). adj. **seminal**.

senility n. The loss or decline of mental faculties, associated with advancing age. adj. **senile**.

sequela n. The consequence; what follows; a disease following and perhaps resulting from, a preceding disease; e.g. pelvic inflammatory disease following a chlamydial infection. pl. **sequelae**.

serum n. The clear, pale yellow liquid that separates out in the clotting of blood.

sex n. Either the male or female of a species, differentiated by reproductive function; also, a general term now emerging describing an erotic sexual act, usually coitus. See **having sex**.

sexual assault Ordinarily, any touching of another person (other than sexual intercourse) for purposes of sexual gratification and without the consent of the victim, or by force or threats. See **rape.**

sexual intercourse Insertion of the penis into the vagina, often to be followed by orgasm of either or both partners. See **coitus, copulation.**

sexual preference A phrase increasingly in use but not yet included in dictionaries, implying acceptance without opprobrium of many forms of a person's sexual behavior, without the infliction of injury or damage. Cunnilingus is stimulation of the female genitalia, orally. Fellatio is stimulation of the penis, orally. Homosexuality is sexual behavior between persons of the same sex. Lesbianism is sexual behavior between females; a lesbian is a female homosexual. Masturbation is manual stimulation of the genitals by self or by another. Sodomy (or buggery) is anal copulation between persons.

sexually transmitted disease (STD) A disease such as gonorrhea or syphilis that is transmitted by sexual contact; a venereal disease. See **venereal disease.**

single parenthood Serving as the unmarried, single head of a family with dependents.

Skene's gland One of two small glands located near the outer end of the female urethra, subject to local infection and abscess formation; not present in all females.

skin n. The organ that is the external or outer covering of the body; also, slang for condom.

skull n. The bony structure which incloses the brain and supports the face.

smear n. A film of a substance such as blood or tissue spread on a microscopic slide for examination.

social disease A disease spread by social contract, esp. a venereal disease, a sexually transmitted disease.

social father The male who raises a child.

social mother The female who raises a child.

societal adj. Social; concerning society or the population.

sociopath n. A psychopath suffering from aggressive antisocial behavior. adj. **sociopathic.**

sodomy n. Generally refers to oral and anal sexual contact between persons; it sometimes includes such acts between persons married to each other; in may include such acts with an animal (bestiality); at one time, called buggery.

soft chancre Slang for chancroid.

sore n. A painful spot or ulcer on the body. adj. **sore.**

speculum n. A mirror; a dilating instrument useful in medicine for the examination of a cavity or passageway.

spermatozoon (sperm) n. The male cell conveyed in semen, which serves to fertilize the female ovum. pl. **spermatazoa.**

spermicide n. A substance or agent that kills the male sperm. adj. **spermicidal.**

spina bifida A serious, congenital defect of the spinal column, in which one or more vertebrae form incompletely, and thus fail to surround and protect the spinal cord; surgery sometimes cures less serious cases.

spine n. The backbone; the vertebral column. adj. **spinal.**

spirochete n. Any of several spiral-shaped bacteria including those that cause syphilis (Treponema) and Lyme disease (Borrelia).

spontaneous abortion See **miscarriage, abortion.**

statute n. A law enacted by the legislature.

statute of limitations A statute limiting the time within which a civil suit may be brought or a criminal charge may be made.

statutory heir A person who, in the case of intestacy, is designated in a statute to be an heir. See **heir.**

statutory rape The crime of sexual intercourse with a female below the age specified in the statute, whom the law presumes conclusively to be incapable of consent; criminal penalties may vary depending upon the ages of the perpetrator and the victim; ignorance of or mistake about age is no defense. See **age of consent, child abuse, consent, rape.**

STD See **sexually transmitted disease.**

sterile adj. Incapable of producing offspring; also, free from disease causing germs or microorganisms. n. **sterility.** See **impotence.**

sterilization n. The act of making sterile.

steroid n. A general name for a group of fatty substances including many hormones, particularly those from the adrenal glands and gonads. adj. **steroidal.**

stillbirth n. The birth of a dead fetus. adj. **stillborn.**

stomach n. Part of the digestive tract that stores, dilutes, and digests food.

stool n. Feces; the excrement from the intestines consisting largely of food residue, bacteria, and cells.

strain n. Slang for gonorrhea.

streptococcus n. Any of various strains of bacteria, existing in pairs or chains, many of which cause diseases such as pneumonia, tonsillitis, scarlet fever, etc. pl. **streptococci.**

streptomycin n. An antibiotic active against many bacterial infections.

stricture n. The narrowing of any passageway such as the urethra in the urinary system; usually due to prior infection.

subclinical adj. A manifestation of a disease too mild for detection by normal tests.

substance abuse The improper or illegal use of a substance, esp. of a controlled substance. See **abuse, controlled substance.**

sue v. To proceed with a civil action to redress a wrong; to prosecute seeking justice.

suit n. An action in court to gain a right or claim.

sulfa n. Short for sulfanilamide; or, as an adj., a drug related chemically to sulfanilamide.

sulfanilamide n. The first of a family of antibacterial drugs of both high potency and toxicity used to treat infections caused by streptococci, gonococci, and similar microorganisms.

superego n. In Freudian psychology, the part of the psyche which criticizes ego and, as conscience, compels moral standards. See **ego, id, psyche.**

support n. The means of a livelihood; a source of sustenance or living, esp. on a scale becoming to one's position in life.

suppository n. A medicated preparation for insertion in the rectum, urethra, or vagina.

surgery n. The instrumental, incisional, or manual treatment of bodily disorders and injuries. adj. **surgical.**

surrogacy n. The act of serving as a surrogate; to act as a substitute.

surrogate n. One who takes the place of another; a substitute.

surrogate parenthood Serving as birth mother; a female in whose uterus is placed a fertilized ovum, which ovum is from another female, and who carries the resulting fetus to term and delivers it.

suture n. The thread or wire used to join, e.g., the edges of a wound, by stitching; the line of juncture of two bones, esp. of the skull.

symptom n. Subjective indication or evidence of a change, disease, or disorder in a patient's condition. adj. **symptomatic.**

syndrome n. Several signs or symptoms which, considered together, characterize a disease or disorder.

syph n. Slang for syphilis.

syphilis n. An infectious disease, usually venereal but sometimes congenital, caused by invasion of a spirochete, affecting eventually almost any organ of the body if untreated. adj. **syphilitic.**

syringe n. A device, composed of a body, a plunger, and a hollow needle, used for injecting medicines or withdrawing body fluids.

systemic n. adj. Affecting the entire body structure; or affecting a system of organs within the body.

tactile adj. Concerning the sense of touch.

tampon n. Material plugged into a body opening to absorb fluid such as blood.

Tay-Sachs disease A hereditary disorder found principally among descendants of east European Jews; the disease is caused by an enzyme deficiency and can lead to mental retardation and death early in childhood; Tay-Sachs disease cannot be treated successfully, but can be diagnosed in utero.

tear n. A drop of the saline fluid which is continuously secreted by glands adjacent to the eye and resembling salivary glands.

tenant n. A person who has a right to property; one who temporarily occupies property of another. See **joint tenants.**

tertiary adj. Of the third stage, order, rank, etc.; third.

testicle n. Gonad. See **testis**.

testis n. Either of two male sex or reproductive glands that produce sperm; located in the scrotum. pl. **testes**.

testosterone n. The principal male sex hormone, produced in the testes; small amounts are produced in the ovaries in females.

tetracycline n. One of a group of antibiotics used to treat numerous infections.

the whites Slang for gonorrhea.

therapeutic abortion The medically induced expulsion of a fetus before it is viable, to protect the life of the female. See **abortion**.

therapy n. The remedial, curative treatment of a disease, or of a disorder such as a mental disorder. adj. **therapeutic**.

threatened miscarriage See **miscarriage**.

tissue n., An aggregate of cells performing a single or related function e.g. connective tissue or membrane.

tort n. A wrong or injury (not a breach of contract) to a person or property, for which damages may be sought by civil action.

toxin n. A poisonous substance; esp. one generated in a plant or animal.

trachoma n. A contagious chlamydial infection of the eye, characterized by granulations, scars, and potential blindness if untreated.

tract n. A region of the body containing related parts or organs.

transfusion n. The transfer of a substance such as blood or plasma from one person, or from a pool or bank, into the bloodstream of another.

transmit v. To pass an infection or disease to another.

trauma n. A physically or psychologically damaging injury.

treatment n. A systematic, curative course of medical or surgical care.

Treponema pallidum The spirochete that causes syphilis.

Trichomonas vaginalis A species of protozoa that causes inflammation of the vagina, urethra, or bladder.

trichomoniasis n. A vaginal, urethral, or bladder infection distinguished by burning, itching, and a yellow discharge. adj. **trichomonal**.

trick n. Slang for trichomonal vaginitis.

trimester n. One of the three three-month periods into which pregnancy is divided. In the *Roe v. Wade* decision about abortion, the U.S. Supreme Court divided the typical 38-week period of human gestation into three parts: the first trimester (approximately the first three months, 12-14 weeks), the time after the first trimester, and the time after viability of the fetus.

trust n. A fiduciary relationship in which property, real or personal, is held and administered by one party (the trustee) for the benefit of another party (the beneficiary).

tubal ligation Blockage of both Fallopian tubes to prevent conception by tying each tube in two places and crushing or removing intervening sections between the ties.

tubal pregnancy A fertilized egg developing in one of the Fallopian tubes rather than in the uterus.

tubule n. A small tube.

tumor n. An abnormal growth of useless tissue, which may be malignant or benign, characterized by excessive proliferation of cells.

TV n. Slang for trichomonal vaginitis.

ulcer n. An open sore (open either on the body's surface or within a body cavity) involving disintegration of tissue and the formation of pus. adj. **ulcerative, ulcerous.**

umbilical cord The circulatory connection between a fetus and the placenta, serving during pregnancy to nourish, and to remove waste from, the fetus.

unjust enrichment A doctrine or principle that a person who unjustly enriches himself at the expense of another should be made to make an equitable restitution.

Ureaplasma urealyticum A group of bacteria or mycoplasmas that may be one of the causes of nonspecific urethritis.

urethra n. The tube (shorter in females than in males) that conveys urine from the bladder to the exterior, and which in males also conveys semen in sexual intercourse. adj. **urethral.**

urethritis n. A painful inflammation caused by an infection of the urethra.

urinary bladder See **bladder.**

urinary tract The organs that together produce and excrete urine.

urination n. The act of excreting urine through the urethra.

urine n. The liquid containing body wastes excreted by the kidneys and stored in the bladder before voiding through the urethra. adj. **urinary,** v. **urinate.**

urology n. The branch of medicine concerned with the study and treatment of the urinary tract in females and the urinary-genital tract in males. adj. **urologic.**

urticaria See **hives.**

uterine infection An infection of the uterus.

uterus n. The womb; the organ of the female in which first the fertilized ovum and later the embryo and the fetus are nourished and developed during pregnancy. adj. **uterine.**

vaccination n. The introduction of killed or altered microorganisms into the body to induce immunity. v. **vaccinate.**

vaccine n. A preparation of weakened or killed microorganisms or viruses, taken by mouth or injection, for the purpose of inducing immunity.

vagina n. The passage in a female lined with mucous membrane, situated between the uterus and the vulva, that receives the penis in sexual intercourse, and through which the newborn baby is delivered. adj. **vaginal.**

vaginal discharge The drainage of glandular secretions and cellular debris from the vagina occurring during the menstrual cycle, or during and as a result of various infections and other disorders.

vaginal thrush Another term for fungal vaginitis; candidiasis of the vagina.

vaginitis n. Inflammation of the vagina caused by an infection or by any of several irritants.

vaginismus n. A painful, spasmodic contraction of the vaginal muscles.

varicose adj. Abnormally dilated or swollen.

varicose vein A vein (i.e. a blood vessel) unnaturally swollen or dilated, often occurring in the legs, esp. of females.

vas deferens A channel carrying sperm from a testicle to a union with the excretory duct of the seminal vesicle. See **vasectomy.**

vasectomy n. Excision of all or part of the duct (the vas deferens) that carries sperm to the ejaculatory duct (and through the penis), the purpose of which is to prevent insemination during intercourse.

VD See **venereal disease.**

vein n. A blood vessel, esp. one carrying blood toward the heart.

venereal adj. Related to sexual indulgence or intercourse; from Venus, the Roman goddess of love.

venereal disease (VD) A disease such as gonorrhea or syphilis that is transmitted by sexual contact; a sexually transmitted disease. See **sexually transmitted disease.**

verdict n. Any decision esp. the decision of a jury. The jury's verdict must be unanimous in criminal cases; the parties may agree in civil cases to accept a majority as the verdict.

vermiform appendix See **appendix.**

vertebra n. Any of the 33 bones that collectively form the spine. pl. **vertebrae.**

vesicle n. A small, fluid-containing sac, bladder, or blister.

viable adj. Able to live and grow; relative to a fetus, able to live and grow outside of the uterus or womb.

violence n. The unlawful exercise of physical force, usually exerted with fury, esp. force intended to result in injury.

virgin n. One (esp. a female) who has never engaged in sexual intercourse.

virion n. The reproductive particle in a virus, capable of infecting a living cell.

virus n. A minute infectious agent, too small to be seen with light microscopes, which can reproduce only within living cells and which can cause a wide range of diseases. adj. **viral.**

visitation rights The rights of a divorced parent, or of a nonparent such as a grandparent, to visit a child; such rights are granted by court order.

vitamin n. Any one of a number of complex organic compounds necessary in the diet for normal body growth.

vomit n. The stomach's contents when expelled through the mouth. v. To eject the stomach's contents, orally.

vulva n. The external part of the female genitalia, including the labia, the mons, and associated glands. adj. **vulval, vulvar.**

wart n. A benign growth on the skin, usually horny, caused by a virus.

wet dream A male orgasm induced by an erotic dream; also called a nocturnal emission.

wheal n. A raised lump on the skin, surrounded by red inflammation, as from an insect bite or hives.

womb See **uterus**.

wrongful act An unlawful act which damages another by infringement upon his or her rights.

yeast infection Another term for fungal vaginitis.

zidovudine n. An antiviral drug used in treatment of AIDS. Formerly called azidothymidine (AZT).

INDEX

233

NOTE INDEX